MOTOCAR
and
RICHARD III
PART TWO

Also by David Pownall

Fiction

African Horse
The Raining Tree War
God Perkins
Light on a Honeycomb
My Organic Uncle *and other stories*

Plays

Music to Murder By
An Audience Called Edouard
The Dream of Chief Crazy Horse

Poetry

Another Country
(Published by Peterloo Poets)

MOTOCAR

AND

RICHARD III PART TWO

by
DAVID POWNALL

with music by
STEPHEN BOXER

FABER AND FABER
London & Boston

First published in 1979
by Faber and Faber Limited
3 Queen Square London WC1N 3AU
Typeset by An Grianán
Printed in Great Britain by
Lowe and Brydone Printers Limited
Thetford Norfolk
All rights reserved

British Library Cataloguing in Publication Data

Pownall, David
Motocar; and, Richard III, Part two.
I. Title   II. Pownall, David. Richard III, part two
822'.9'14   PR6066.0995

ISBN 0-571-11340-0

MOTOCAR

a play about Rhodesia

For John Edward Adams and the company

CHARACTERS

Motocar
Inspector Pickerill
Sister Donahue
Nurse Symonds
Doctor Lewis

NOTE

The play benefits from being played without an interval, though provision for a break is made in this text. Running-time is 100 minutes.

Seating-plan for Motocar's meeting is seen as below:

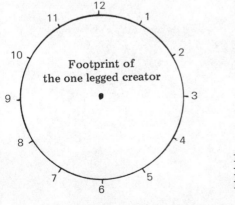

Footprint of
the one legged creator

1 Kissinger
2 Price
3 Silveira
4 Lobengula
5 Moshesh
6 Sophocles
7 Mzilikasi
8 Moffat
9 Mauch
10 Tshaka
11 Victoria
12 Monomotapa

Motocar was first performed by Paines Plough at the Traverse Theatre Club, Edinburgh on 1st February 1977, directed by Edward Adams. The cast was as follows:

MOTOCAR	Joe Marcell
PICKERILL	Eric Richard
DONAHUE	Fiona Victory
SYMONDS	Diana Kyle
LEWIS	Stephen Boxer

ACT ONE

*The linen-room of a mental hospital for Africans near Salisbury,
Rhodesia. Shelves of clean, folded sheets. Six big wickerwork
laundry baskets, some of them open, with dirty sheets, pyjamas,
overalls, underwear, spilling out into jumbled piles on the floor.
Graffiti on the walls and shelves—VOULEZ-VOUS VORSTER?
BISHOP, BLESS US ALL. ZZZZZZZZIMBABWE. VAKOMANA
WELKOM HOME. GO MUGABE GO. BLACKSMITH. GENEVA.
ZANU. ZAPU. STEVE BIKO WILL SELF-DESTRUCT IN FIVE
SECONDS.
Telephone rings, then stops.*

MOTOCAR: [*Off*] Dlhodlhodlho.
PICKERILL: [*Off*] Tulake, tulake...Quiet, man, keep the noise
    down for Christ's sake, this is a hospital...you've got to keep
    quiet in here.
MOTOCAR: [*Entering with PICKERILL*] Dlhodlhodlho.
PICKERILL: Now that's enough, man...Stop it...[*Sees the room.*]
    What's this? This can't be the right room. That bloody fool on
    the switchboard has sent us to the wrong place...it would be
    nice for them to get something right, just once in a while eh?
    Just once in a while...Come on, back we go.
    [*PICKERILL turns MOTOCAR round to leave. Enter SISTER
    DONAHUE.*]
DONAHUE: What's going on here?
MOTOCAR: Head-ring.
PICKERILL: We've been sent to the wrong place...
DONAHUE: Did he do this? [*To MOTOCAR.*] Did you make this
    mess? I've been after you for a long time my lad...
PICKERILL: No, he's with me...We were sent here by mistake...
DONAHUE: Three times this week this has happened. I've had
    enough of it. D'you hear? Stupid kids playing games! Why are
    you holding hands with him?
    [*PICKERILL holds up their handcuffed hands.*]
PICKERILL: He's a prisoner. I've brought him here for a psychiatric
    examination.
DONAHUE: Is he dangerous?
PICKERILL: They're all dangerous at the moment, aren't they?
DONAHUE: Don't ask me. All I know is they're making my life
    impossible. This country's had it. Politics you see, politics.
    Everything has to be politics. Even my houseboy, politics in the

9

morning, politics at night...if he breaks a plate, it's politics.

MOTOCAR: Dlhodlhodlho...

DONAHUE: Ach, and the same to you. You tire me out. They haven't got half a brain between the whole lot of them, have you? Have you got a brain in there?

MOTOCAR: Head-ring. Head-ring. Head-ring.

PICKERILL: Tulake! Well, I'd better find out where the right room is for this examination. It's not here, that's for sure.

DONAHUE: Who told you it was here?

PICKERILL: The boys on the switchboard...

DONAHUE: Don't believe a word they say. That whole gang out there in reception are loafers. They think they're very amusing. I'd fire the lot of them tomorrow. Politics again, you see, very cocky, very uppity.

PICKERILL: He said room twelve. Do you think they can count that far?

DONAHUE: Well, this is room twelve.

PICKERILL: They've just cocked it up. Well, you can't expect them to get a simple thing like that right can you? That's a real intellectual problem, getting a room number right. I'll go back and sort it out. Come on, chamware.

DONAHUE: Hold on, I'll find out for you. I'll ring through and ask. [*Looks for phone.*] Very funny, very grown-up sense of humour the boys have here. Do you feel confident about being governed by a bunch of clowns and bullies? They're trying my patience. And I came here for a quiet life. You can laugh if you like. [*Finds phone under a laundry basket.*] See what I mean? Children. Tiny-tots.

PICKERILL: You have got some right jokers here.

DONAHUE: [*Dialling O*] Sister Donahue here...Yes, it's me...That's right...Will you be quiet and let me talk?...I have a person here...

PICKERILL: Inspector Pickerill—to see Doctor Grobbler.

DONAHUE: Yes...Inspector Pickerill...yes, he's a bwana...yes...you remember him, do you?...Now that's remarkable in itself... Which room did you send him to?...Twelve? Now why twelve? It's the linen-room...Doesn't that strike you as odd? Very funny, what a gentleman you are...Why did you send him to the linen-room you bloody fool?!...Oh...Doctor Lewis...er...all right ...[*Replaces receiver.*] This is the right room. We're very short of space. Beds everywhere.

PICKERILL: Oh...I'd better wait then. I think I'll take these cuffs off. They're playing hell with my wrist...Stand still... [*PICKERILL unlocks the handcuffs.*]

DONAHUE: Are you sure that's wise?

PICKERILL: I've been with him all day. He's not violent...

DONAHUE: Yet. I don't trust any of them. I've been burgled five

10

times in the last three months, insulted every day at work, jostled in the street...They're out of control. I used to like this place, I did, after Belfast it was Paradise...

PICKERILL: Things change.

MOTOCAR: Things change. Things change.

PICKERILL: All right man, I don't need you chipping in. Go and sit down. Like I do. Go on, sit, squat.

MOTOCAR: Half a brain. Which half?

DONAHUE: What's that you said?

MOTOCAR: Catch a train. Witchcraft.

DONAHUE: You think you're so clever, don't you? I'll leave you to it, Inspector. I'd like you to imagine trying to work with fifteen hundred comedians like this, real thickheads. I'll tell Doctor Lewis you're here. He's the Deputy Chief Psychiatrist. He's running the place, now, trying to...

PICKERILL: Actually, my appointment is with Doctor Grobbler.

DONAHUE: Doctor Grobbler's in Johannesburg. He flew down last night. He's gone for good, run, run, just left us to it. That's what I feel like doing. I don't really want to go back up there on the wards. Isn't that terrible? I'm doing no good you see, they hate me. I can feel it coming out of them, real hate. I thought I could take everything they handed out but I can't. Not an atom of gratitude. [*Pause*] Well, no good putting off the evil day. Where else would have me, eh? I liked it here. I liked everything about it. You could live with some self-respect, until now.

PICKERILL: I know what you mean.

DONAHUE: They're children. It's going to be Peter Pan land. A fantastic country like this given to a gang of kids. We'll be governed by thugs and murderers...Christ, it makes me so mad... Ah, to hell with it. Have you got a cigarette? Let them break the place up for a while...

MOTOCAR: I want my head-ring. I have worked hard for it, quietly in small rooms, with books. No man has worked harder. Do not deny me my head-ring.

DONAHUE: [*Taking a cigarette and light off PICKERILL*] See, here you have a future Prime Minister. We got so tired, you know. This place is on its last legs. They don't care. Let the grass grow over the roof. That's what one of the orderlies said, let the grass grow over the roof. They don't care. They don't care about their own people. Death, madness, they've always been very close to the African. He has no respect for human life. That's why they live like they do.

PICKERILL: Yes...I see what you mean...er, my instructions were to have the prisoner examined by Doctor Grobbler specifically. If he's not here any more I'd better check with headquarters in Salisbury to find out what I should do...

DONAHUE: [*Giving cigarette to PICKERILL*] Here, you finish this.
I'd better push on. Would you like some tea?

PICKERILL: That would be great. I take sugar, he doesn't.

DONAHUE: Oh. If you see Doctor Lewis would you ask him to ring
the Sister's desk on ward seven. Tell him it's urgent. There's a
couple of jokers up there who reckon they're conspiring to
commit suicide together, a pact, you know what I mean? Just
say—amytal...amytal—we need amytal. It's the Mpesu brothers.
Twins. Now isn't that sweet?

PICKERILL: Is it all right if I make a call on that phone?

DONAHUE: Sure. Just dial O for the operator and ask for a line.

PICKERILL: Thanks.

DONAHUE: You're welcome. Well, back into the breach, dear
friends.

[*DONAHUE exits.*]

MOTOCAR: What a charming woman.

PICKERILL: Don't you be insolent. Keep quiet now while I make
this call. [*Dials O.*] Operator? A line to Salisbury please. No...not
Salisbury England...Don't try and be funny, boy, it doesn't
wash with me...[*Pause. Then he dials.*] Hello. Stan...hello, Stan?
Yes, Ray here...Look, there's been a mix-up here...Who is that?
You again...man, have you been listening in on my call?...Man
I'll be out there chop chop and sort you out...Why can't you
give me a line?...What meeting?...All right, all right...But just
cut the fun and games, eh? This is government business...Give
me a line as soon as you can. [*Replaces receiver.*] This really is
a madhouse you know. They're all bloody mad. You see what
you've achieved here? Complete confusion.

MOTOCAR: You mentioned a meeting.

PICKERILL: Yes, he says all the lines are being used for this
meeting, for the delegates.

MOTOCAR: What were their names?

PICKERILL: I can't remember. This is a real cock-up. I drive all the
way from Marandellas and find the psychiatrist has buggered
off to Johannesburg. Typical.

MOTOCAR: Was one of them called Mzilikasi?

PICKERILL: I don't know. They were probably talking bullshit,
anyway.

MOTOCAR: Do you know if they perform the split-brain operation
in this hospital?

PICKERILL: I shouldn't think so. To split a brain you've got to
have a brain to split.

MOTOCAR: May I have another cigarette?

PICKERILL: Man, you're costing me money. This is the last.

[*PICKERILL gives MOTOCAR a cigarette, lights it. As soon as
MOTOCAR takes the first draw, DOCTOR LEWIS enters.*

*PICKERILL snatches the cigarette out of MOTOCAR's mouth
and puts it under his shoe, with his own.*]

PICKERILL: Hello, are you the deputy?

LEWIS: Yes, my name is Lewis. [*Shakes hands with PICKERILL.*]
Inspector Pickerill? [*Bends down and picks up the flattened
cigarettes, dropping them in a waste bin.*]

PICKERILL: Right...er...this is the prisoner...
[*Telephone rings. LEWIS is nearest, he answers it.*]

PICKERILL: I think you'll find that call is for me.

LEWIS: Hold on, operator. [*To PICKERILL.*] Are you Mr Mzilikasi?

PICKERILL: No. Isn't the call for me?

LEWIS:[*To MOTOCAR*] Is that your name?

MOTOCAR: Yes.

LEWIS: Then you'd better take the call.

PICKERILL: His name is not Mr Mzilikasi.

LEWIS: Well the call is for someone of that name. Perhaps there are
two of you? Try elsewhere operator.
[*LEWIS replaces the receiver. Enter NURSE SYMONDS with
two cups and a sugar-bowl on a tray and some folded sheets
under her arm.*]

SYMONDS: Excuse me. Is this your tea? Did you ask for it?

MOTOCAR: Ah, the first-year essays. Good. Put them in my in-tray.

PICKERILL: Yes. The sister said she'd arrange for it. Is that all
right, Doctor?

LEWIS: Certainly.
[*SYMONDS gives MOTOCAR his tea.*]

MOTOCAR: No sugar, thank you. He does, three.
[*SYMONDS gives PICKERILL his tea. He puts in three sugars,
self-consciously.*]

LEWIS: You know Doctor Grobbler is in Johannesburg?

PICKERILL: Yes, it's a nuisance. I've got to get this okey looked at.

LEWIS: Why are you bothering?

PICKERILL: Those are my instructions.

LEWIS: I'm afraid that I am not prepared to do it. Don't leave,
Martha.

SYMONDS: I have to get back. Did Grace see you about the amytal
for the Mpesu brothers? They've been terrible today. You've no
idea the things they get up to...

LEWIS: I don't think we have any amytal left.

PICKERILL: I'm not sure that I was going to ask you anyway.
[*Telephone rings. He answers it as he speaks.*] Headquarters said
Doctor Grobbler—extension 68—Stan? Ray here...I've run into
a problem...The proper doctor is away and this place is—very
busy, they can't fit me in...Yes...I realize that...I can only ask...
No, I saw nothing on the way here...Where've they been sighted?
Christ, that many?...Right, I'll wrap it up as soon as I can and

get out of here...Yes, don't worry. I'll be back before dark...
I'll keep a look out for terrorists...No, man, they can't shoot
straight, you know that, not at a moving target...See you, Stan...
[*PICKERILL replaces the receiver, takes an envelope from his
pocket and draws out a paper.*] Right, Doctor, we haven't got
much time.

LEWIS: May I ask what is that?

PICKERILL: The request from the Ministry for the examination.
His name is Motocar, as far as we can tell...

SYMONDS: Motocar. The names they get given, Motocar.

PICKERILL: Please be as quick as you can. I've got other work to
do.

[*PICKERILL offers the paper to LEWIS, who does not take it.*]

LEWIS: And we haven't of course. How long has he been in custody?

PICKERILL: About six hours.

LEWIS: [*Angrily*] After eleven, twelve years of bungling, stupidity
and arrogance, we can streamline a case like this in six hours,
yet I am kept waiting for decisions, supplies, staff...all of them
urgent. Have you any idea how impossible life has been made
for us here? This hospital is falling apart. I'm trying to run it
single-handed. I simply haven't got time for this kind of thing.

SYMONDS: All the nurses are getting out as fast as they can. We
can't keep track of what's going on. Half the patients are
moving their families in. Right, I'm going back to Grace...Don't
forget the amytal, Doctor, we must have it...

MOTOCAR: At a place called Lôwê, twelve miles north of Machudi,
is a hole in the dry river-bed. On the rocks there are hundreds
of footprints made by the first creatures ever to appear in the
world. [*Hands the cup and saucer to SYMONDS.*] The hole
itself is the footprint of the one-legged creator who retired into
the mark of his own life when he was disappointed with what
he had made.

PICKERILL: Will you examine him?

LEWIS: No. Martha, I want you to witness my refusal.

SYMONDS: All right Doctor, but make it snappy. Grace is expecting
me back. I only popped out for a minute. She can't manage by
herself up there.

LEWIS: You can go as soon as we've sorted this out...

PICKERILL: This is a government order, an order. We have to have
him examined.

LEWIS: Not by me. It is quite pointless. We are two weeks away
from Independence.

PICKERILL: How do you know he's political?

LEWIS: Because you are here, and it is obviously urgent. Under
normal circumstances we do our examination at the prison
hospital. I'm not interested in the details. The answer is no. Nor

14

will I allow any other member of my staff to examine him.

SYMONDS: Let me go now, Doctor. Grace will kill me!

LEWIS: She'll just have to wait!

PICKERILL: Doctor, this is a serious business. This man is accused
of a crime, an offence against the law. We reckon he killed a
man. But he doesn't act normal. We can't follow him. He could
be acting...

[Enter DONAHUE with a bundle of dirty sheets, shouting.]

DONAHUE: Christ Almighty, Martha, can't you leave him alone for
a minute? I thought I told you to get back straight away? Did
you get any amytal? Did you give her any amytal for the Mpesu
brothers, Doctor? They're tearing the recreation room apart.
Ping-pong I said, play ping-pong. They're using the bats as
hatchets...

LEWIS: Grace, please...we have a problem here...I'll be with you
shortly...

DONAHUE: [Moving to go] Then we'll leave you to it. Come on,
Martha.

LEWIS: Don't go.

DONAHUE: What are you talking about? I've got to go...and Martha
as well.

LEWIS: Grace, the Inspector here is trying to force me to give a
psychiatric examination to a political prisoner. I am refusing. I
want your support, please.

PICKERILL: You want her as a witness as well?

LEWIS: Isn't that the way you work?

PICKERILL: Isn't it your job to stand in for your chief?

LEWIS: That is correct.

PICKERILL: Then you've got to examine him. It's your responsibility.

DONAHUE: [To MOTOCAR] Don't smile like that. Sorry, Doctor.
All right, we'll stay. Okay, Martha, we'll take our break now. I
declare this our break-time. You two lads do your stuff now.
Let chaos reign.

LEWIS: [To PICKERILL] I am rejecting that particular responsibility. Whether this man is sane or mad is not something we
can judge within the present situation. It is not a psychiatric
opinion you are seeking, it is a political attitude.

PICKERILL: Doctor, all I want is a scientific opinion...

DONAHUE: You can have my opinion if you want.

LEWIS: Grace!

DONAHUE: We're still in our break-time. Do you mind if my junior
and me have a smoke while we witness this confrontation? It's
impolite, I know, but we do need it. The whole place is falling
to pieces you see. Nothing is worth it. The orderlies don't take
a blind bit of notice of what I say to them. Have you got your

15

little tin of equipment there, Martha my love? Roll us a couple while we're waiting. Carry on now Doctor. Stick up for yourself. Don't let him walk all over you now, the great bully. You've let us down you know, you soldiers and all. I never want to see another soldier as long as I live. You're useless, useless.
[*SYMONDS rolls two cigarettes.*]

LEWIS: Grace, I'm sorry that I have to ask you to do this but I must protect myself. Do you think I should examine him?

DONAHUE: [*Throwing the bundle of sheets on the floor*] I don't care! Why should I care?
[*Pause. DONAHUE sits on a basket next to SYMONDS and they light their cigarettes.*]

MOTOCAR: Dodadodadodadoda. I'd better get down to it. Yawn.

PICKERILL: Shut up man. Give me time to think. I don't know what the hell to do.

LEWIS: I suggest you simply take him back and tell your superiors of my decision.

PICKERILL: I can't do that. He goes on trial in two days.

LEWIS: You're actually going to put him on trial ten days before Independence?

PICKERILL: Of course. He committed a crime, we think.

DONAHUE: Why don't you just shoot him?

PICKERILL: [*Angrily*] I don't like that kind of talk from a woman! It's not right.

DONAHUE: He's a terrorist isn't he? You don't bother to keep them when you catch them. What's so special about him?

PICKERILL: I didn't say he was a terrorist. He might be. And what the army does out there in the bush is their affair. You've no right to assume that I agree with it...

MOTOCAR: Dodadodadoda...

PICKERILL: Shut up damn you! Three hours in that bloody jeep I had of you, now keep quiet!

MOTOCAR: I will get married within the next year and join the ranks of the ama-Doda. The ama-Tjaha is for boys, not men.

LEWIS: [*To PICKERILL*] Will you go now?

PICKERILL: No. I'll have to ring through and ask headquarters what steps to take. Will you give me your reasons?

DONAHUE: He's given you his reasons. He thinks it's a waste of time.

PICKERILL: I asked him not you.

SYMONDS: That's what he said. It's a waste of time.

LEWIS: Don't get involved, Martha. I'll do the explaining thank you.

SYMONDS: And I just sit here? Okay, I'll do that. My ward is going to be in chaos but I'm needed here. He's smiling again, Sister.

DONAHUE: What are you smiling at? Have you wet yourself, you bad boy?

MOTOCAR: [*Sniffing up the smoke of their cigarettes*] Waaah! Waaah!

DONAHUE } [*Laughing*] Waaah! Waaah!
SYMONDS }

PICKERILL: [*Picking up the telephone and dialling O*] Hello... operator...get me a line will you?...Twenty minutes? Why so long?...All right...[*Replaces receiver.*] Twenty bloody minutes. This is ridiculous!

[*MOTOCAR explores the shelves, picks up a clean folded sheet.*]

LEWIS: In that case we shall just have to leave you to it, Inspector... [*Goes to leave.*]

PICKERILL: No way. You stay right where you are!

LEWIS: I have a hospital to run...

PICKERILL: [*Barring his exit*] I said stay where you are. You'll have to wait.

LEWIS: [*Flaring up*] I'm sick to death of this stupid behaviour and I am leaving to get on with my work. You have no right to stop me.

PICKERILL: [*Standing aside*] Okay, go on, leave. [*Pause*] As long as you realize you'll be committing an offence.

DONAHUE: Oh, he's a hard man this one. I bet the hairs on his chest would put a scrubbing-brush to shame. You're a great lad, one of the best.

LEWIS: Grace, it would be helpful if you would let me deal with this. [*To PICKERILL*] Get out. Get out of this hospital. Go on, get out.

PICKERILL: You are obstructing the law. You are obstructing a policeman in the execution of his duty. You are defying a government instruction.

DONAHUE: Sounds like a hanging job to me, Doctor.

LEWIS: You can't make any of that stick. It's completely fatuous and I shan't let it pass. I will report you for this. [*Pause*] What a sense of priorities you people have. But you must have your own way, oh yes, to hell with all the rest. I am appalled by your behaviour...atrocious stupidity...this place won't survive and who will wonder?

MOTOCAR: [*Over SYMONDS's shoulder, looking at the folded sheet in his hands*] What did I give you for your last essay? C-minus? I hope this will be better. Before we even leave the first paragraph, I don't remember saying that I thought Ernest Hemingway was the best African writer of his generation. Whom did I say it was? Wilbur Smith surely? Robert Ruark perhaps? Maybe Doris Lessing?

PICKERILL: Not now, eh?

MOTOCAR: Yours was no better. If you get any more than D-plus for this garbage you'll be doing well. When did I say in any tutorial of mine that 'The Imprisonment of Obatala' had

17

anything to do with Samuel Beckett? Samuel Beckett is alive
and doing well. Why should I usher him through the portals of
the University of Pittsburg?

PICKERILL: Knock it off will you?

MOTOCAR: [*Throwing the sheet on the floor*] I give out the titles
here!

PICKERILL: Pick those up!

MOTOCAR: What easier task for you than to write an essay when
there are no texts to study? All Africans are illiterate. What is
the point of writing for them?

PICKERILL: I said, pick those up. You put them there now pick
them up.

LEWIS: [*Picking up the sheets*] Don't worry. Relax. The answer is
still no. No. No. No.

PICKERILL: Are you saying there are practical difficulties?

LEWIS: No. I am just refusing to go through the motions.

PICKERILL: Then you're breaking your contract.

LEWIS: My notice of resignation went in a week ago.

PICKERILL: That doesn't make any difference. You're still bound
by your contract.

MOTOCAR: [*Inhaling the smoke again*] Waaah!

DONAHUE
SYMONDS } Waaah!

MOTOCAR: Eater of men. Stabber of heaven. Calf of a black cow.
Thunderer. Black pig. May I marry?
[*DONAHUE and SYMONDS laugh.*]

PICKERILL: What are you girls smoking?

DONAHUE: We're witnesses.

PICKERILL: You run a pretty shambolic hospital here.

LEWIS: Put it out.

DONAHUE: We're still in our break.

LEWIS: I said, put it out!

DONAHUE: [*Pause*] What did this African do then?

PICKERILL: You heard what he said, put it out! You talk to me
about witnesses. That's illegal, you know. And in a hospital, a
bloody mental hospital. Christ, no wonder we're in the mess
we're in. You've got chaos here, d'you know that? [*Telephone
rings. PICKERILL answers it.*] No! There's no one called Mr
Moffat here! Stop putting wrong calls through to this number
man...Now get me that line...Never mind about the cost centre...
tsetsha! [*Pause*] Hello? [*Rattles the cradle.*] Hello...Bastard,
he's cut me off. [*Replaces receiver.*] Absolute chaos you've got
here. What an organization.

SYMONDS: Do you want to hear my latest, Grace?

DONAHUE: She writes songs, beautiful songs. I've told her to send
them to a publisher or a group but she never does.

18

SYMONDS: I've only got the words, no music.

DONAHUE: Sometimes I think your words are better than your music and then I think, no, the music is better than the words.

LEWIS: Not now if you don't mind.

SYMONDS: I haven't even got a title for it yet...

PICKERILL: Christ Almighty.

DONAHUE: I feel ten times better. This morning I felt as though my heart was going to crack right open but that's gone away now. Come on, Martha, let's hear it.

SYMONDS: They're not interested.

MOTOCAR: I am, I am. Creative writing is my speciality. I trained up a whole generation of American novelists and taught them the ways of Zen, Captain Marvel and moose-hunting.

SYMONDS: Of what a perfect length is the African day.
            How strange is sleep. How odd is darkness.
            Here on the high plateau the air is cool
            And my plants grow to eight feet and more
            Outside the dispensary door.

MOTOCAR: Excellent. I particularly liked the juxtaposition of a spatial mystery, e.g. 'how odd is darkness' with a vegetable conundrum, '*my* plants', i.e., plants which are an extension of my own being becoming eight feet and more viz., outstripping my physical height while extending my consciousness through genial hallucinations affecting Time. I like, yeah, I like it.

SYMONDS: Thanks.

[*Telephone rings. PICKERILL snatches it up.*]

PICKERILL: No...there's no meeting, no palaver here...

MOTOCAR: [*Rushing for the telephone*] Ngi Nzula mine!
    [*PICKERILL stops MOTOCAR in his tracks with a punch.
    MOTOCAR doubles up and kneels on the floor, groaning.
    PICKERILL carefully replaces the telephone.*]

PICKERILL: That's quite a switchboard you've got there. Same as everything else in this bloody place. Help me with him.

LEWIS: Don't sit him up, he's better off where he is. I think I'll go now. The Mpesu brothers will have massacred each other...

PICKERILL: [*Loudly*] He was found on the Inyanga mountain two hours after old chief Senzangakona was shot in his own chicken-run. He had this case in his hand. He was wearing a suit and a hat. He only got as far as me because it was a couple of journalists picked him up. No gun. No alibi. He told me in the jeep on the way here that he had just graduated from Bible college in Glasgow.

DONAHUE: Now you mention the Bible. We've got thousands of men who know about the Bible in here. Do you know that there are seven hundred sects of the Christian church in Africa alone? If he went to Bible college you can assume he's mad.

MOTOCAR: No, no, he got it all wrong. I only did a short course...
[*Sits up.*] What a punch. Did you see that punch? It only
travelled six inches.
[*PICKERILL helps MOTOCAR to his feet.*]
PICKERILL: Go on then, I'll take him back. [*Pause*] Have you
applied for your exit visa yet, Doctor?
MOTOCAR: May I have that cigarette now? You hurt me.
LEWIS: Would you care to amplify that question?
PICKERILL: [*Giving MOTOCAR a cigarette and lighting it for him*]
You are leaving I think. You are one of those who are leaving.
You've got to be. There's a look about you. Yes, you're on your
bicycle all right.
DONAHUE: Don't start, Martha.
[*SYMONDS cries quietly.*]
LEWIS: Did you hear that? He threatened me. I will report you for
that.
PICKERILL: Why should the government help you if you won't do
the job you're paid for? Yes, it's a threat. Think about it.
LEWIS: You heard what he said, Grace? Martha? He threatened me.
DONAHUE: Did I? Grobbler's gone. He won't be back. You're
going. What's going to happen to us? Who's going to run this
place? And look at poor Martha, a picture of misery. You know,
she believed all that crap you talked, Doctor. Doctor Lewis is a
great bleeding heart you know. Famous throughout the wards.
LEWIS: Come on, Martha, snap out of it.
SYMONDS: I renewed my contract because of you. I'm stuck here
for three years.
LEWIS: You can always break your contract.
PICKERILL: That's your prescription for everything, isn't it?
SYMONDS: You did say we might go away together at one time.
DONAHUE: Oh, he's moved on from there. It's all over, Martha my
love. Don't say he didn't warn you. Impossible he said. You
were an aberration. He must marry a woman of his own faith.
Isn't that right, Doctor? A big, juicy Jewess. And he can't abide
people who change their religion for emotional reasons.
LEWIS: You don't seriously expect me to bow to this kind of
pressure do you? The Ministry of Health will cancel any
attempt to interfere with the granting of my visa.
PICKERILL: The Ministry of Health is run by Africans, Doctor,
which is why you are leaving.
LEWIS: That is not so.
DONAHUE: Don't lie. Of course it is.
LEWIS: I'm leaving for personal reasons. I have always supported
the idea of independence and majority rule.
PICKERILL: Ideas are ideas. He's an idea. I'm an idea. These two
women are ideas. Why don't you support us?

LEWIS: Don't be deliberately naïve, Inspector. You and your short-
    sighted colleagues have seen to it that there can be no rapport
    between the races here. It will take at least ten years before any
    kind of trust can be re-established. I cannot wait that long
    before I have the right conditions in which to do my work. You,
    and prejudiced bureaucrats like you, have forced me to abandon
    this country. And when it does collapse, and when there is
    wholesale butchery as we had in the Congo and Uganda and
    Nigeria, I would like you to remember who created the situation.
    You have brought ten years of profiteering and unwritten apart-
    heid in this country at the expense of the entire future, and for
    that you can have my utter contempt. You are blind, ignorant
    bigots.
PICKERILL: Have you quite finished?
LEWIS: I could go on, but, I think, to little effect. You don't listen.
    People like you never do.
PICKERILL: I can't choose, Doctor. I have to listen. That's what
    I'm paid for. But don't expect me to like you for it. Now, listen
    to me, let me put it quite straight to you. Either you give this
    prisoner a psychiatric examination, or you don't leave Rhodesia,
    or Zimbabwe.
LEWIS: You can control the former, but not the latter.
PICKERILL: You'd be surprised Doctor. I'm actually staying on.
    Now isn't that a turn-up for the books? And you know, they
    will probably promote me as well. That couldn't be because I
    know my job and do what I'm paid for—it must be because
    they're all crazy these black people. Don't you think so?
    [Pause]
LEWIS: I give up. Don't tell me any more. That's it. [Pause] Do
    they want him certified insane?
PICKERILL: Who's they?
LEWIS: Your superiors.
PICKERILL: Any particular colour you fancy?
LEWIS: I don't care who they are. Just tell me exactly what they
    want. I want to satisfy their needs to the letter. There's no
    problem, none whatsoever. They shall have what they want. I
    will give you a certificate to say he is mad, and another
    certificate to say he is sane. You can then use which one you
    like.
PICKERILL: Don't be so bloody stupid!
LEWIS: Not at all. I am in no position to behave with any honesty.
    You need a certificate to get him either on or off the hook, I'll
    give you one, two! Integrity has nothing to do with this
    situation. I will be corrupted, gladly. Use me.
PICKERILL: I want a proper test.
DONAHUE: [Waking SYMONDS] You're sleeping with your mouth

21

open. Aaron here finds that off-putting. Do you ever wake up and find her sleeping with her mouth open?

LEWIS: You may go now.

SYMONDS: I had a dream.

DONAHUE: Martha had a dream, Doctor. I don't think we'll bother to go back on the wards. Half an hour without us and there is absolute confusion. They'll be eating each other.

SYMONDS: In my dream I was allowed to break my contract and keep my termination benefit, and my pension accrual. I was allowed currency clearance and I drove to Johannesburg but you'd gone to Australia. So I drove to Australia. Sod!

[*Telephone rings. LEWIS picks it up, beating PICKERILL to it.*]

MOTOCAR: That will be for Moshesh.

LEWIS: [*Pause*] Are you Moshesh as well?

MOTOCAR: Am I Moshesh? Have I got the face of the BaMokotedi?

LEWIS: [*Into phone*] No, he's not here... [*Replaces phone.*]

MOTOCAR: Ah, he is, he is. [*Stands up.*]

PICKERILL: Sit down man! Who keeps making these calls?

MOTOCAR: North of the Black Umfolosi River lived the Ndwande under Zwide; south of it the Mthethwa under their chief Dingiswayo; in between was a small clan ruled by Senzangakona. They called themselves the Zulu and many had loud voices.

PICKERILL: Who is Moshesh?

MOTOCAR: He is at the meeting.

PICKERILL: What meeting?

MOTOCAR: He is at this meeting.

PICKERILL: There's no meeting here.

MOTOCAR: Oh yes, there is. First a prayer-meeting. This is the prayer-meeting. We are all praying for a miracle. Then we will have a meeting to discuss my marriage in terms of the miracle. What is the greatest miracle in the Bible? Ah, not too good on religious knowledge. You will get Z-minus for that.

LEWIS: Shall we get on with it? The examination will only take fifteen minutes.

MOTOCAR: Certainly Doctor.

[*MOTOCAR bustles about, shifting SYMONDS and DONAHUE and making a throne to sit on. PICKERILL follows him.*]

PICKERILL: Hey, hold on. Have you got any friends in this hospital?

MOTOCAR: Only you.

LEWIS: What's the matter?

PICKERILL: He's tied in with that joker on the switchboard some-how. Bloody mind-readers or something.

DONAHUE: Inspector, those men are monkeys. Don't take any notice. Come on. let's get this over with...

PICKERILL: Nurse, would you go and check that switchboard for me? All I want to know is whether it's the regular operator. Just have a look, you don't have to say anything.

LEWIS: Inspector, the switchboard here is notorious...

PICKERILL: It's more than that at the moment. It's psychic. Will you do that for me, Nurse?

SYMONDS: If it will get me out of here, with pleasure. Shall I get some tea?

MOTOCAR: Please, no sugar. [*SYMONDS exits.*] Now, check the list...Mzilikasi...Moshesh...Lobengula...should I have asked Lewanika and Khama? A quick rehearsal of my opening address before the doors of the conference chamber are opened... [*Clears his throat.*] There will be delegates here who will recall in their opening speeches the Festival of the First Fruits when, as young men, they slew a pitch-black bull with their bare hands. As we speak a common language, or common enough, there will be no need for simultaneous translation though old pictures may be circulated in brochure form. Before it is too late, I ask to be married. I ask permission from this great assembly to wed; not the woman of my choice but the woman whom you give to me, from any land, anywhere. I think that hangs quite well together. Yes. [*Pause*] You're not the brightest group to have in a tutorial, not by a long stretch. At times you irritate me most profoundly. Try this. Compare the affirmative cynicism of Chinua Achebe, James Joyce and the bare bones of Sophoclean drama. Criticize, discuss and explode all myths connected with Oedipus and the Easter Rising of 1916. What was Doctor Johnson's dictionary definition of the equator? That which goes round the earth once and twice round the neck of Africa. You have all failed and I will recommend your removal from this place of learning, by force if need be, children, dogs and cattle! Out! Out of my sight you halfwits, morons!

PICKERILL: [*Whispering*] Any the wiser? He was like this all the way here. Complete rubbish. I don't understand a word of it.

LEWIS: Inspector, please don't interfere. It might be better if you left...

MOTOCAR: No! That man is my friend. My bodyguard. Would you leave your Emperor unprotected? Think of the risk of assassination, a *coup d'état*. He stays, he stays...

LEWIS: Very well, very well.

DONAHUE: See, somebody loves you. Does that make you feel good?

MOTOCAR: Niga mina lo wetu!

LEWIS: What is he saying?

PICKERILL: He wants the brief-case. He says it's his friend.

LEWIS: Give it to him then.

PICKERILL: I'll have to remove a few things first.

[*PICKERILL opens the brief-case and takes out a big stone.*]

DONAHUE: Is that a stone? What does he lug a great stone around for?

MOTOCAR: I want everything.

PICKERILL: Not the stone, chamware, not the stone.

MOTOCAR: Tell this masepa hela to give me my goods! And those papers. I must have those papers.

PICKERILL: You keep a civil tongue in your head. What do you want the papers for?

MOTOCAR: Every meeting must have papers. Haven't you found that out for yourself? Agendas, minutes, essays, notes.

DONAHUE: Well, a real smart alec. Do you have to have stones in your meeting boy? African confetti for your wedding?

LEWIS: Grace, I'd be obliged if you wouldn't interfere. Give him what he wants.

[*PICKERILL hands MOTOCAR the papers and the stone. MOTOCAR takes out twelve books and puts them in a neat pile, checking their titles.*]

LEWIS: Are you prepared to give me any background to his offence?

PICKERILL: Alleged offence. I told you before, we think he shot a chief. Well, the old man used to be a chief, poor bastard. I knew him from when I was on bush patrol.

LEWIS: Any idea why...

[*Telephone rings. PICKERILL runs across, grabs it.*]

PICKERILL: Voetsak man! [*Slams the receiver back.*] Bloody bastards!

DONAHUE: Temper, temper.

LEWIS: And who was that one for?

PICKERILL: For Mr Sophocles, a Greek gentleman. Was he at the meeting? I'm going to sort these bastards out.

[*PICKERILL strides off. MOTOCAR carries the stone above his head. Lays it down reverently. Shouts, crashing, confusion from off.*]

PICKERILL: [*Off*] What do you want? Hey...Christ man...get off...

LEWIS: [*Coming across*] What's going on out there? Inspector, are you all right?

[*PICKERILL is catapulted back on stage, blood on his mouth, his jacket half-off, his shoulder-holster empty.*]

PICKERILL: Bastards...They took my gun...they jumped me...

LEWIS: Grace, this is an emergency...Alert the security...

[*Explosions, gunfire, ululations off.*]

DONAHUE: It's a bomb! It's a bomb! Clear the building!

[*DONAHUE runs for the door. PICKERILL pulls her down.*]

PICKERILL: Get down!

[*LEWIS throws himself flat, DONAHUE continues screaming, struggling. Pop-soul music off.*]

MOTOCAR: [*Holding a book aloft*] Opposite me, at six o'clock, a

24

chief and apostle of words, James, son of Apheus, Sophocles.
Welcome, welcome. Will you sit down? [*Places the book.*] Good
of you to have come so far...
[*Enter SYMONDS wearing a grotesque African mask, a transistor
radio under one arm, a cardboard-box in the other. She charges
into MOTOCAR's arms. He grabs her, spins her round.*]
Do you think you can love me? Do you think you can settle
down with me?
[*MOTOCAR takes the radio and cardboard-box away from her
and she collapses into DONAHUE's arms.*]
DONAHUE: Martha...is that you Martha...Oh, your poor face, your
poor pretty face...[*Heaves at the mask.*] Keep still and I'll get
this off you...
SYMONDS: [*Pushing DONAHUE away*] No, no! Don't touch it!
MOTOCAR: Oh, it suits her. Beautiful. The masks my people make
are prized the world over.
PICKERILL: Shut up! Just stay put, keep down...
[*SYMONDS and DONAHUE whisper, whimper, argue.*]
MOTOCAR: [*Holding another book aloft*] Here is an old comrade,
Father Gonçalo de Silveira, a creeping Jesuit. Is the black
produced by burning blacker than the black produced by an
absence of white Christ in the washing? [*Places the book.*] At
three. [*Stands by SYMONDS.*] Hm...isn't she beautiful? Would
you like to have her, Inspector?
PICKERILL: Get down, man. Stop that shit!
MOTOCAR: [*Returning to his throne, switching off the radio on the
way*] They must sit in the correct order of precedence. At a
round table this poses its problems...
PICKERILL: Get down off there!
MOTOCAR: When Monomotapa sits, all sit.
PICKERILL: Motocar, do as you're told...
MOTOCAR: Monomotapa. Monomotapa. You don't listen when a
man gives his name.
PICKERILL: Do you want to get yourself killed, you stupid bastard?
MOTOCAR: I will not be killed, but you will unless you behave
yourselves and try harder with your homework.
[*Telephone rings. MOTOCAR gets off his throne and crosses to
it.*]
PICKERILL: Leave it! Don't touch that phone...
MOTOCAR: [*Picking up telephone*] Hold on. [*To PICKERILL.*]
Don't be anxious, Inspector. It will only be the news that
Lobengula's indunas are back from London. I have asked them
to address the meeting and give their report. [*Into phone.*]
Sorry about that. There is some confusion in here...yes...oh yes,
they will help me, I'm sure they will...[*To PICKERILL.*] You
will help me with my meeting, won't you? [*Into phone.*] Yes,

very readily. They are most kind, most sympathetic…They should keep away from the door which is now being locked until the meeting is over…[*To* PICKERILL.] Do you understand that? You must not go near that door. All right? [*Into phone.*] Yes, give us a few minutes to sort ourselves out and we'll get started in here…[*Replaces receiver.*]
[*Lights fade to blackout.*]

ACT TWO

Lights snap up on the characters in the exact positions they were left at the end of Act One.

MOTOCAR: Know much about the brain, Inspector?

PICKERILL: So you are a bloody terrorist. That's nice. And you've brought your mates along for the ride. Perfect. All I need. Christ, I know you bastards like a soft target but I thought you might have more dignity than to attack an undefended mental hospital for your own people!

MOTOCAR: Do you know anything at all about the human brain, Inspector?

LEWIS: Please...Inspector. Don't react. [*To MOTOCAR.*] Now I think you want us to help you with your meeting. Is that right?

MOTOCAR: What shape is the human brain, Inspector?

LEWIS: Am I correct? You seem most anxious we should help you.

MOTOCAR: Yes, yes, in a moment. First things first. Inspector, seen from the left, what shape is the human brain?
[*Pause*]

DONAHUE: Either you men do something, or I'm just getting up and going out that door with Martha...

PICKERILL: Stay put! You're not going anywhere. [*Pause*] Shit.

LEWIS: Answer him, Inspector.

PICKERILL: I don't know. I really don't. You tell me.

DONAHUE: This child is terrified out of her wits, she can hardly breathe. She won't let me take this mask off...

LEWIS: Grace, sit still, give me a moment! Be sensible!

MOTOCAR: Look closely at the Doctor, Inspector. He is a long-headed Caucasian type. He has a truly European skull. Yours is similar. Mine, rounder, like a football. The human brain, seen from the left side, is in the shape of Africa. It is in that continent that my meeting must take place. Here. Inside this bucket of old bone. Hard outside, soft in.

PICKERILL: Man, that's very interesting, but...to more practical matters. All I want is this—those hooligans called off. You're not going to achieve anything here...

MOTOCAR: See, Ethiopia is swallowing and mastication. The Congo is hearing. Nigeria is conscious thought. The Sahara, salivation. Egypt, sensory elaboration. Tunisia, tongue. Namibia, perceptual judgement. South Africa, contralateral vision, Rhodesia, visual and auditory recollection.

DONAHUE: [*Furiously*] Will you do something with him, you hopeless pair of dummies? Get him out of here at least...

LEWIS: That is extremely perceptive of you. Yes, I enjoy that...er... that analogy.

MOTOCAR: Now, my problem is this. How do I get inside that brain to have my meeting. Obviously I must operate. This is the right kind of place. You do lobotomies here I believe. So, there must be tools. I will have to shave the scalp, incise the skin, drill several holes, then out will come the bone-saw, a little square lifts out. Trepanning, I love that word, reminds me of looking for gold. Trepanning.

PICKERILL: Man, just drop all that. You can't touch anyone in this room. That is out of the question. Now, these girls are very frightened. The Doctor has work to do. You and I must get back [*Pause*] I accept that you are sick. If that's enough, call off your friends, eh? Ring the switchboard.

MOTOCAR: Well, if you're not going to let me do an operation, I'll just improvise. [*Picks up the cardboard-box which SYMONDS brought in.*] A poor substitute. I could do brain surgery. My hand is steady enough. So, trepanning, trepanning, trepanning. [*Takes off the lid.*] Hmmm. Just as I thought. Phew. This one has gone off.

DONAHUE: [*Screaming*] Will you stop this fucking nonsense before I go mad? You, Motocar, whatever your bloody name is, you're crazy. Do you understand? You're not right in the head. Now... let us help you, properly...like we're trained to do...I'm sorry, but give us a chance...

MOTOCAR: Maggots.

DONAHUE: Let my girl take that thing off her face.

MOTOCAR: No, she has to keep it on for the meeting. This brain needs cleaning out. If we're going to have a meeting in it we need the right atmosphere. Jesus, the maggots have laid eggs. Look. [*Takes out a plastic container of capsules.*]

LEWIS: Where did you get those?

MOTOCAR: Who is short of amytal in this hospital?

DONAHUE: Thieving bastards. We needed those!

MOTOCAR: And you may have them. [*Brings out three more containers and places them at the four compass points around the stone.*] Doctor, how many pills have you made my people swallow? How many sedatives? How many bromides? One for you. One for you. One for you. And one for you.

PICKERILL: For the love of God, stop this now.

MOTOCAR: Inspector, you were silent on the subject of the brain. I suggest you extend that curfew to God as well. My people opened their mouths for you, Doctor. Have you got the courage to do the same for them? Who is curing whom in this house of

28

strange medecines? Now, the meeting. I could do with some
help in ushering the delegates to their places. [*Picks up books.*]
Here is our Chief Lobengula whom I usher to four. Now,
Inspector, I want you to take Carl Mauch, gold prospector, to
nine.

PICKERILL: Here?

MOTOCAR: Exactly. Now, Doctor—a doctor for a doctor. Will you
take Doctor Matthew Price of London to two o'clock? [*Gives
him one book, then another.*] And next to him our Lobengula
at four.

[*LEWIS quickly places the books on the clock.*]

I think I'd better do the next one myself. Protocol demands it.
Here, on my right, at eleven o'clock, Simon Peter Victoria,
Queen of Great Britain and Ireland, Empress of India...no
mention of Africa...[*Places the book.*] How good of you to
come all the way to my barren and miserable land. [*Picks up the
sheaf of papers.*] Sister, see these papers? Would you be so
good as to place them for us? This delegate, our man at one
o'clock, is still in flight. He will need them as reference
documents as soon as he joins us. When he touches down at the
airport I will have to pop out to meet him. He will expect it.

DONAHUE: Why should I be interested in your bloody papers?

MOTOCAR: [*Sternly*] These are the minutes of the meetings which
Doctor Henry Kissinger, the American Secretary of State, has
had with Mr Vorster, Mr Smith, Mr Kaunda, Mr Nyerere, Mr
Callaghan, Mr Everybody, about the settlement of the Rhodesian
question. [*Thrusts the papers under DONAHUE's nose.*]

LEWIS: Do as he asks, Grace. Do as the Emperor asks.

DONAHUE: Where do you want him? [*Takes the papers.*]

MOTOCAR: Can you not tell the time? Here!

[*DONAHUE takes the papers and returns to SYMONDS.*]

MOTOCAR:[*Taking a pile of books*] Simon Zelotes Mzilikasi here,
at seven, next to his friend Bartholomew Robert Moffat of
Kuruman at eight. Old chamwares, mates. They work well
together. Here at five, Thomas Moshesh, wise Chief of the
BaMokotedi of the Sutho nation, already sitting at ease, resting,
thoughtful of great questions. [*Pause*] Are we all here? No,
here is an empty seat, at ten o'clock. What does the name read
Doctor.

LEWIS: I cannot see from here.

MOTOCAR: It is a difficult spelling. Hm. We are missing one delegate.
He may still be outside. We will have to wait for him. [*Pause.
Phone rings.*] That will be him. He is here. [*Answers the phone.*]
Yes, we are ready, all set. Has he arrived? Oh...I see. [*Replaces
the receiver then places two books at ten o'clock.*]

PICKERILL: Who's the double-helping?

MOTOCAR: Eater of men. Stabber of heaven. Calf of a black cow.
The great elephant is late. We have had a ship-to-shore cable
from Tshaka the Terrible. There have been contrary winds all
the way from the West Indies. He is having a difficult passage.
[*MOTOCAR stands in front of each book on the clock in turn,
bows, greets the delegate. Dialogue continues over.*]
PICKERILL: [*To DONAHUE*] What is the amytal stuff?
DONAHUE: It's one of the strongest tranquillizers we use here.
Twenty-five will kill you.
PICKERILL: Jesus Christ. They're ruthless these bastards. Half of
them are schoolchildren, schoolchildren with bloody machine-
guns.
DONAHUE: You couldn't beat them though, could you?
PICKERILL: In this terrain? No chance. They're back in the bush in
five minutes...
MOTOCAR: May we have silence please? I am about to give my
opening address. [*Beckons SYMONDS over.*] Come on.
PICKERILL: Yeah, yeah, sorry. You carry on. What a balls-up.
LEWIS: We have no choice but to co-operate. Come on. Make the
best of it.
[*Pause. MOTOCAR mounts his throne, sits down. SYMONDS
below.*]
MOTOCAR: You see before you a simple bachelor who has much to
share. My empire stretches from the Gwai River in the east, all
the way west to the Indian Ocean: from the Zambesi River in
the north to the Limpopo in the south. It is a great, wide, rich
land, the heart of Africa. Now I wish to take a wife. It is
customary to consult all interested parties as to whom should be
my partner.
PICKERILL: Somebody as mad as yourself! I've gone as far as I'm
going...
SYMONDS: You can't get out of it. They're serious. [*To MOTOCAR.*]
We are ready. Which one of the delegates would you like to
speak first?
MOTOCAR: The Jesuit, the Portuguese Jesuit. Will he rise?
SYMONDS: Will you do it, Doctor?
LEWIS: Oh, I see...you want me here? [*Moves to three o'clock.*]
Three o'clock.
[*Pause*]
MOTOCAR: Well? What are you apostle of? Olive oil? Cork?
Port-wine?
LEWIS: Exactly what do you wish to know?
MOTOCAR: What does your God say about marriage?
LEWIS: He says it is a good thing.
MOTOCAR: That's not what you told me last week.
LEWIS: Didn't I?
30

MOTOCAR: Saint Paul. You said Saint Paul said that a man should only marry if he has to. So, the question is, do I have to?

LEWIS: Yes, I suppose it is.

MOTOCAR: Not much use then are you?

LEWIS: It appears not.

MOTOCAR: Time for my favourite story of yours, out of your thousands and thousands.

LEWIS: Which one is that?

MOTOCAR: The matje mhope story. [*Picks up the stone, weighs it in his hand.*]

LEWIS: I do not know that story.

MOTOCAR: You do not know the white stone story?

LEWIS: That is one I do not know.

MOTOCAR: The Whitsun story? No? [*Turns to DONAHUE.*] Queen Victoria will know it. Tell him the Whitsun story. What is Whitsun all about?

DONAHUE: I have forgotten.

MOTOCAR: The Queen of Ireland has forgotten Pentecost?

DONAHUE: I have heard of it.

MOTOCAR: [*Putting the stone down*] You have heard of what you celebrate? That is sound practice. [*Pause*] My favourite story, told me by this Jesuit gentleman here, concerns the descent of a holy bird from heaven, bringing the gift of tongues to twelve Apostles that they might speak to men of all nations. Strange that you should have forgotten the best story in the Bible. [*Pause*] So, my Portugoose, you have nothing sensible to say about my marriage? Nothing at all?

LEWIS: I am sorry that I am not able to help.

MOTOCAR: I have killed men for less.

LEWIS: Yes.

MOTOCAR: You want to die? Are you as tired of life as I am?

LEWIS: No, I do not want to die. I wish to live.

MOTOCAR: Then you can fold the sheets.
    [*Pause*]

LEWIS: The sheets?

PICKERILL: Do as he says.
    [*LEWIS picks up some dirty sheets.*]

MOTOCAR: No, not those. Those. [*Points at a pile of clean sheets.*]

DONAHUE: They're folded already.

MOTOCAR: Do you want to die? I have absolute power. I ask you again. Do you want to die?

DONAHUE: No!

MOTOCAR: A sheet that has been folded may, under certain circumstances, usefully be folded again. Take one end...[*Helps LEWIS with the sheet, taking an end across to DONAHUE, then involving PICKERILL.*]...break it out. Three ends, not four.

31

Fold it, fold it. [*To PICKERILL.*] Sophocles, a delta, delta! [*He organizes them so they form a triangle with the sheet.*] Now, lift it. Raise it! [*To SYMONDS.*] Babiyane! Whistle, whistle. [*SYMONDS tries to whistle through the mask, fails.*] No, no, a long whistle, like this. All of you whistle. Come on, whistle. [*Whistles*] I can't do it for you. I am in the reception lounge contemplating the fact that a one-legged creator is nothing but a God who limps. Whistle, more, more. A long sustained blast. That's it. [*Holding the sheet aloft, they whistle one long high note.*] Henry is coming, Henry, Henry, Henry, the Kiss-in-the-ringer who will save those who cannot save themselves. He will establish the first Feast of the Handover amongst his Chosen People. The great bird descends. The earth shakes. The Holy Spirit flies down on his wide American wings, landing on runway twelve! [*They lower the sheet slowly, stretching it taut so it vibrates.*] Here at the airport a large crowd has gathered. As the dove alights, tongues of flame streaming from its throat, the people burst into spontaneous song, holy, holy, holy! The whole of this land dwells in the shadow of his swept-back wings. His jet-engines go into reverse-thrust to assist it with the braking process. On the tarmac the twelve Apostles suddenly speak their minds in all the languages of Man. [*Pause*] Speak...please...speak up for me. Help me. Speak, I beg you, speak.

[*Pause. They let go of the sheet. MOTOCAR paces over it, beseeching, tense, expectant. Then they all speak together.*]

SYMONDS: Spiritus Domini replevit orbem terrarum alleluja: et hoc quod continet omnia, scientiam habet vocis.

DONAHUE: M'anam go raibh sé millteanach fuar ar an loch.

LEWIS: Kai tēn potheinen patrida paraschou autois,
     Paradeisou palin poiōn politas autous.

PICKERILL: Basopa zimvwana yena hayi lahlega; noko wena lahlegile yena mina zo tshaya wena.

MOTOCAR: [*Delighted*] That's it...now don't lose it, stay with it, hold on...[*Sweeps the sheet up and puts it round PICKERILL's shoulders, steering him to four o'clock.*] Lobengula, the indunas have arrived back from London. Will you see them now?

PICKERILL: Me? You want me to do him?

MOTOCAR: You are him. You are my friend. Squat. [*PICKERILL obeys.*] Assume your seat. [*Going to SYMONDS and taking her hand, bringing her across to PICKERILL.*] My wife here is suddenly very old, very frightened...an old, old man who has been a long way across the sea. Lobengula is tired after his heavy lunch in the luxury dining-suite of the conference centre. [*Rattles a container of amytal capsules under PICKERILL's nose.*] Wakey-wakey! We have a report from Babiyane. Queen

Victoria...[*Turns to DONAHUE, puts a container of capsules at her feet.*]...you won't mind if this is given in your presence? I'm sure you won't be embarrassed. [*Pause. MOTOCAR puts another container at LEWIS's feet and the final one at SYMONDS's.*] Now, speak, Babiyane, induna of Lobengula. And keep it short. The delegates are likely to nod off at this hour of the day. [*Pause*] Well, cat got your tongue? We are waiting. Very nervous. Let me help you. Let me help you all. [*MOTOCAR picks up the container of capsules at LEWIS's feet and puts them in LEWIS's hands, then pushes the container to the edge of LEWIS's lip. Pause. Then he tilts the container to one side so it rattles, then back, smiling at LEWIS, nodding his head in rhythm. LEWIS cottons on, relief flooding his face. He shakes the container in the right rhythm. MOTOCAR moves on to PICKERILL, DONAHUE. They have already understood and are shaking their containers. MOTOCAR laughs, urges them on, bounding around the clock. Rhythm rises. Light changes. SYMONDS starts to tremble, breathes very deeply, then screams. PICKERILL, LEWIS and DONAHUE buckle, groaning, breathing very deeply.*]

First Babiyane, tell us how you were received by Queen Victoria. What is she like? [*LEWIS starts to crawl from three to nine, DONAHUE stumbles to eleven.*]

SYMONDS: [*In a clear, altered voice*] When she entered the room where we were waiting, I was stricken with fear and I crouched on the floor with my hands on my stomach and the Queen laughed and said, 'Rise, rise O Babiyane!' And I stood up and saw, hau! She was very small, very, very small, no higher than a calabash of beer, but terrible to look at—a great ruler.

MOTOCAR: You have a letter, Lobengula, sent from this terrible Queen. What advice does she give?

PICKERILL: [*As Lobengula*] I have no letter.

MOTOCAR: We know. The letter that the Queen sent you was intercepted by Cecil Rhodes. It will be too late. It made him very angry. He wanted to drop it in the sea. It was a good letter.

DONAHUE: [*As Victoria*] Dear Friend, as you are now being asked by many for permission to seek gold and dig it up in your country, we would have you be wary and firm in resisting proposals that will not bring good to you and your people.

MOTOCAR: And why do these men seek gold in my empire, Mr Carl Mauch?

LEWIS: [*As Mauch, German accent*] When I saw the white reefs of auriferous quartz glistening in the sun I was startled by the conception of the wealth before me. The vast extent and beauty of these goldfields is such that I stood transfixed, struck with wonder and amazement at the sight. These goldfields are greater than those of California and Australia put together.

MOTOCAR: And Babiyane, what did you see in London?

SYMONDS: We saw many things. We saw a display of the new British machine-gun. We saw the vaults of the great bank where all their gold is kept. We wondered why they must come to Matabeleland to gather more when they had so much already —and we were given none as gifts, a thing we thought miserly. What Matabele would take a distinguished guest to his kraal to show him a herd of cattle and not offer the guest one beast? Also we saw the men of the Aborigines Protection Society.

MOTOCAR: Were they men of God, these men of the Aborigines Protection Society?

SYMONDS: Some were, some were not.

MOTOCAR: Was one of them our delegate here, Doctor Price, also of London...[*PICKERILL takes off the sheet, goes to two o'clock.*] Did you meet Babiyane Doctor?

PICKERILL: [*As Price*] I did not. It was after my time.

MOTOCAR: You are a political divine, so I am told.

PICKERILL: A fighting parson, sir. A man of the people. On the 4th of November, 1789, I preached a goodish sermon in which I asserted that by the principles of the Glorious Revolution of 1688, the English people had acquired three fundamental rights: 1) To choose their own governors; 2) To cashier them for misconduct; 3) To frame a government for themselves.

MOTOCAR: Are the people of England aborigines Doctor?

PICKERILL: They are aboriginal in England.

MOTOCAR: Are these the rights of an aborigine or an Englishman?

PICKERILL: They are the rights of those who have fought for them.

MOTOCAR: Do those who have fought for them have any spare rights for others, especially aborigines who are not English?

PICKERILL: What rights they have are all spoken for. Other men in other lands must find their own rights.

MOTOCAR: So the export of English rights is prohibited?

PICKERILL: Impractical. They do not travel well, like some wines.

MOTOCAR: Oh some do, some do...They keep their flavour as well as any claret.

PICKERILL: Which may I ask?

MOTOCAR: Prospecting rights. [*Pause*] And now I am pleased to announce that two old comrades, men who can see into each other's minds, Moffat, the missionary and Mzilikasi, the Chief of the Matabele—[*DONAHUE joins PICKERILL. Arm in arm they go to seven and eight.*]—have got their heads together. [*They sit down on the floor. PICKERILL slumps forward.*] Mzilikasi, I know that you are sick, I know that you are old and find it difficult to speak, but can you remember what you said to Mr Moffat here on that first day when he entered your kraal with his Bible in his hand? [*PICKERILL beckons MOTOCAR to come close. He whispers into his ear.*] What? Yes...yes...this is what you said...I, Mzilikasi, say this to my friend in the presence of all my indunas. Mr Moffat, sir, I do not want to hear the cry of a white man's child. I do not want to hear the bark of a white man's dog. I do not want to hear the lowing of a white man's calf in Matabeleland. [*Pause*] And then Mzilikasi, after Mr Moffat had cured you of a great sickness and saved you from death? What did you say then? Ah yes...[*PICKERILL whispers again.*] My heart is all white as milk. I am still wondering at the love of a stranger who never saw me. You have loved me. You have fed me. You have protected me. You have carried me in your arms. I live today by the stranger of another nation. [*Pause*] Mr Moffat, that love, the love you showed the dying Chief, was not your own was it? Time and again you said it —Christ it is who loves you through me. Moshesh—[*LEWIS moves to five.*]—on this point you have made a minority report. You suggest that I marry a white woman but make her accept my ways. Persuade us. Make the meeting accept your proposal. The floor is yours. [*LEWIS stands in the centre of the clock by the stone.*] What have you got against Christ?

LEWIS: [*As Moshesh*] Moffati ka e re Morimo ki khosi ka ena...

MOTOCAR: Mosheshi, these others have used the gift of tongues to speak up for me. Return their favour. Use the Apostles' international language. Show you are prepared to bend that far.

LEWIS: Moffat said that God is a chief like any other chief. I treated this with disdain. I am a king and I will not put myself under the authority of another, especially this ambitious man Christ. I have my kingdom and he has his. Let him stick to his and I will stick to mine. And if he, or any of his people, wish to live with us then they must accept our ways. I am also suspicious of this man Christ as I hear that he orders the brains of men to be drunk from cups and I will have none of that impurity near me, nor the eating of human flesh.

[*PICKERILL, DONAHUE, SYMONDS and MOTOCAR cheer, applaud.*]

MOTOCAR: The delegates are rising in their seats...a standing ovation for Moshesh, well done, well done, well said! Splendid speech!

[*The cheering subsides, then the clapping, suddenly PICKERILL pitches forward. Then LEWIS. DONAHUE gropes her way to a basket, sits down. Pause.*]

LEWIS: [*As LEWIS, very tired*] Have you finished with us now?

MOTOCAR: No.

LEWIS: How else can we help you?

MOTOCAR: I would like to provide some entertainment for my

guests.

LEWIS: Entertainment?

MOTOCAR: You know…singing and dancing.

DONAHUE: Well get on with it…

MOTOCAR: No, I mean these chaps here. I want them to do it.

PICKERILL: Oh piss off…no…

LEWIS: [*Struggling to his feet*] What exactly would you like us to do?

MOTOCAR: Izigizumba.

LEWIS: Izigizumba.

MOTOCAR: Come on, you both know it. You've sung and danced it
round a thousand camp-fires as Boy Scouts and on countless buses
coming home from rugby games. Izigizumba, when you are ready.

PICKERILL: That's it…this is as far as I go…

LEWIS: [*Half-crawling*] Izigizumba zumba zumba [*Pulling at
PICKERILL's arm.*] Come on Inspector…izigizumba zumba ze…

PICKERILL: Man, have you got no pride left?

MOTOCAR: Dance! Dance!

[*PICKERILL and LEWIS, hanging on to each other, circle, stamp
and sing.*]

PICKERILL: Izigizumba zumba zumba
LEWIS: Izigizumba zumba ze
             Hold him down you Zulu warrior
             Hold him down you Zulu chief chief chief
             [*Repeat*]

MOTOCAR: Enough! [*LEWIS and PICKERILL collapse.*] Magnifi-
cent. The delegates are delighted. A wonderful performance. Thank
you, thank you. Now all that remains is the closing hymn and the
meeting will be over. You all know it. I could ask for no better choir.
Sing for me, sing for us all, Nkosi Sikalele Afrika, God Save Africa.
[*Pause. LEWIS starts to sing, very shakily. The song comes out
of their exhaustion, one by one until they are singing together.
MOTOCAR joins them.*]

ALL: Nkosi sikalele Afrika,
             asiphakhamise igama layo,
             yamukhele inkuleko zethu,
             Nkosi sikalela,
             thina bantwana bayo.
             [*Repeat*]

             Hoza moya, hoza moya, sikalela,
             hoza moya, hoza moya, sikalela,
             hoza moya, hoza moya, unqwele,
             he-usi sikalele
             he-thina bantwana bayo.
             [*Repeat*]

[*From outside the final lines of the chorus are heard, sung by*

36

*hundreds of voices. Pause. Telephone rings. MOTOCAR crosses
and picks it up.*]

MOTOCAR: [*Covering the mouthpiece*] Excuse me a moment. And
thank you, thank you. [*Uncovers mouthpiece.*] Yes, a great
success. They have advised me to marry a white woman, the
African White Butterfly, if I can catch her. Yes, I am very happy,
very happy indeed. Thank you all. Thank all my friends. Now, I
am sending one of my helpers out for the file. Give it to her
without question. [*Replace receiver, returns to throne.*] Queen
Victoria, will you go and get the file for me? [*Pause. Sits on the
throne.*] You have all done wonderfully well. I thank you from
the bottom of my heart.

DONAHUE: Me? Go out there? You're joking!

MOTOCAR: Do as you are told, woman.

DONAHUE: They'll make me wear a mask. They'll touch me!
[*MOTOCAR descends from the throne, puts a hand on
SYMONDS's head. She stiffens.*]

MOTOCAR: And how do you like your new face?

SYMONDS: It hurts. It's cutting into me.

DONAHUE: You brutal sod! Keeping her in that ugly rotten thing
with wire cutting into her head...

MOTOCAR: I thought I told you to go and get the file.
[*DONAHUE exits.*]
The land goes to those who want it most. There are no friendly
spirits. We are grazing animals, we wander where we like. Empty!
Empty!
[*He flings open a basket and tears the contents out, hurling them
all over the stage.*]
We were hollow men for a hundred years. [*Pause. He grins at
PICKERILL.*] Do you remember the bit in the *Merry Wives of
Windsor* when Falstaff hides in the laundry-basket? I like that
bit. You, get in.

PICKERILL: What for?

MOTOCAR: I like to be reminded of Shakespeare. His greatest comic
character was, of course, Othello, or Shylock, but I still have a
soft spot for old Falstaff. Hop in.

PICKERILL: No.

MOTOCAR: You don't feel in character?
[*Pause*]

PICKERILL: I'll do you a deal. I'll get in if you let her take that thing
off her face.

MOTOCAR: Oho, then I'll do you a deal. She can take that thing off
her face if you'll get in and let me sit on top.

PICKERILL: Christ, you're a cockeyed person. Why do you want to
do that?

MOTOCAR: You are luggage. You look like luggage. You are luggage.

37

Get in! The sister is out there...do you wish to jeopardize her life? Get in! [*PICKERILL climbs into the basket. MOTOCAR sits on top.*] Here I am, at the railway station, sitting on my luggage. Here I am at Kennedy Airport, Heathrow, Charles de Gaulle, Moscow...sitting on my luggage. All right in there?

PICKERILL: Hurry up man, there's not much room in here. These sheets stink.

LEWIS: May I take the mask off now?

MOTOCAR: I never break my word.

[*LEWIS takes the mask off SYMONDS.*]

MOTOCAR: Listen, my luggage is talking. Tired of movement. Tired having no home. It creaks with despair. The sound of the exhausted swallow forever in flight across all the oceans of the world. Just how I felt in my migrations. In and out of those rooms, rooms, libraries, libraries, welcomes, scholarships and fellowships, universities and societies, pamphlets and magazines, causes and demonstrations, sympathies and arguments. Me and my luggage, oh, a brilliant student! A special case, send him abroad, fly him away. I said goodbye to my father and his empty hundred years, goodbye to the Matabele, goodbye to the Mashona, goodbye to Africa, and went away to write the truth about this country. One day I would return and set the record straight, in peace like Noah's dove after the flood, bringing hope. I failed. I wrote no book. I could not start, I could not finish. I was too bitter to stay on the page and burned through the paper, brown vinegar. [*Furiously attacks the basket, kicking and punching it, spinning it round. Muffled shouts from inside.*] So how much have we got in there? How many pairs? How many animals two by two? Or is it Pandora's Box, full of infectious diseases and misery? I should have left my luggage behind! Thrown it overboard!

LEWIS: Don't you think you've had enough fun out of him now?

MOTOCAR: Man is a detestable animal!

[*Enter DONAHUE, knocked about, dishevelled, her hair down, panting, with file.*]

DONAHUE: So he is!

MOTOCAR: It is an act of wisdom to see Man as a detestable animal. [*Grabs a heap of dirty sheets and clothing.*] Look at this, blood, snot, piss, shit, vomit, yagh! [*Throws them away.*] I ask, who is it detests Man with such passion? What other creature bothers to hate him? God? Never, one-legged or two. From my studies I deduce that only Man has the gift of self-disgust. Push those baskets together.

LEWIS: How do you mean?

PICKERILL: [*From in the basket*] What's going on? Have you finished?

MOTOCAR: [*Assembling the baskets in an upstage-downstage line*]
Put them end to end, come on, quickly, Tshaka is returning.
[*They obey, pushing the baskets into a line.*]

PICKERILL: Don't you get me going now...Let me out of here...

DONAHUE: What's the game now?

MOTOCAR: Come on, build, build...

PICKERILL: Have you finished now...We had a deal man...It's not
much bloody fun in here...

MOTOCAR: [*Opening the lids of the other baskets*] Now all get in,
all of you. Doctor, you in the forward compartment, the women
aft. You will be fed once a day and let out for a short promenade
in the early evening...

LEWIS: I refuse...I won't do it...

MOTOCAR: Get in the hold!

LEWIS: I flatly refuse. You must stop tormenting us.

MOTOCAR: [*Grabbing LEWIS*] Get down in the hold!

LEWIS: [*Struggling*] No! Don't force me. Let me get in by myself.

PICKERILL: Bloody mad filthy bastard!

MOTOCAR: Hurry, hurry! [*Slams the lid down, fixes the fastener.*]
Now you girls...

DONAHUE: I'm not getting in there. You can do what you like to
me but I'll look you in the face while you're doing it. I don't
think there's an ounce of madness in you, not an ounce. You
want to see us all dead...
[*SYMONDS makes a bolt for the door. MOTOCAR catches her
and carries her to the baskets, puts her in. DONAHUE gets in
of her own accord. MOTOCAR closes the lid.*]

MOTOCAR: The wind is getting up, a strong east wind veering to
south-east. All aboard! Cast off!

PICKERILL: Let me out of here or there'll be trouble! You'll get me
going! I'm getting cramp...
[*SYMONDS and DONAHUE can be heard crying. LEWIS mutter-
ing. PICKERILL groaning throughout the next sequence.*]

MOTOCAR: [*Taking off his shoes and tee-shirt*] Tshaka the Terrible,
Tshaka the Zulu, never got to my meeting. His ship was slow,
weighed down by a pale, shining cargo. He has crossed the Atlan-
tic back to Africa. The West Indian experience fades in the
following wind. The long shame is over.

PICKERILL: Damn you, you mad bastard, I'm choking in here...

MOTOCAR: Check the bills of lading. Forward hold, man-slaves of
thought, thinkers, justifiers, watch them closely. Centre hold,
man-slaves of action, chain them tight. Aft hold, sisters of mercy,
mothers, women-slaves, all as white as ebony. [*Gets on top of the
central basket—PICKERILL's—now he is Tshaka.*] An impi
salutes us from the fortress. We return to the mouth of the Black
Umfulosi River. Home! Home! Africa! I see the coast. After a

39

hundred years I am coming home, a rich man. Do you hear me? This is Tshaka speaking. Through the roar of the breakers, the threads of the sea-mist, do you hear me? [*Drums reply from outside.*] Open the estuary. Reverse your spears. Lower your shields. I, Tshaka, the son of Senzangakona, am coming home. [*Drums reply.*] Oh, the smell, the smell of the land. After so long at sea with this cargo of stars. Who was it wanted a white wife? Who wanted a skilful servant? [*Drums reply.*] I have wives and women here in the hold. I have doctors and witch-doctors. I have priests and policemen. I have administrators, governors, bishops, generals, judges, chairmen, do you want them? [*Drums reply.*] I have technologists, sociologists, anthropologists, economists, ecologists, nuclear physicists, dieticians, paediatricians, engineers...Do you want them? [*Drums reply.*] How will you treat them? Like men? Like the animals we are? And where will they live? [*Pause*] Becalmed again. I am waiting at the harbour mouth. There is still sea between us. We are drifting. The anchor will not hold. My ship drifts in the current. No rope is long enough. Stop me. I am losing sight of Africa. I am being carried round the Cape of Good Hope by contrary winds. I will never see Africa again.

[*MOTOCAR gets off the baskets, exhausted, heart-broken. Silently he opens the baskets one by one, PICKERILL's being last. LEWIS, SYMONDS and DONAHUE get out quickly and quietly, but PICKERILL burst out in a tremendous rage, faces MOTOCAR.*]

PICKERILL: Don't you get me going! Don't mess me around! Cut it out...Just watch it, eh...Leave me alone...bastard...Don't you get me going again...Don't you wind me up, you stupid munt! [*Pause. MOTOCAR glares back fiercely.*] Forgive me.

LEWIS: Forgive him.

PICKERILL: Forgive me. Forgive me. Forgive me.

MOTOCAR: I do, I do.

PICKERILL: I'm very sorry. I apologize. Forgive me. Forgive me.

MOTOCAR: Give Doctor Lewis the file.

[*DONAHUE hands LEWIS the file. PICKERILL crumples, leaning back against the baskets.*]

PICKERILL: You got me going...Don't get me going like that again, please...Don't wind me up...

MOTOCAR: Fold the sheets.

SYMONDS: Us?

MOTOCAR: Yes.

[*SYMONDS picks up a clean sheet.*]

PICKERILL: Not those sheets, the other sheets.

SYMONDS: But they're dirty sheets...

PICKERILL: Don't you understand? He wants dirty sheets.

40

DONAHUE: Is that right?

MOTOCAR: Yes, I'm only interested in dirty sheets. Come on, girls, tidy up, fold...

[*DONAHUE takes a dirty sheet from a basket and gives the other end to SYMONDS. They start to fold it.*]

MOTOCAR: Will you read the cards for Senzangakona, Albert, please Doctor? Begin at the beginning. Fold girls, fold, keep going...

LEWIS: These are all for Senzangakona...

MOTOCAR: A busy man, my father. His case history is in your hands.

PICKERILL: Senzangakona? The old man was your father?

MOTOCAR: Come on, girls, tidy up. Fold these sheets for me.

[*SYMONDS and DONAHUE work through the basket of dirty sheets as the file is being read out by LEWIS. The sheets get progressively greyer.*]

LEWIS: Senzangakona, Albert. Tribe, Matabele. Born Bulawayo 1900 approx. Religion, blank...

MOTOCAR: A Christian at Christmas, a Mohammedan at Ramadan.

PICKERILL: You killed your own father. Bloody hell.

LEWIS: First date of admission: 19th June 1922, suffering from depression and acute paranoia. Incipient schizophrenia.

MOTOCAR: A self-governing colony, that's what they asked to be in that year, those farmers, those miners, a self-governing colony. Father did not understand the western concept of self. There is a white self and a black self.

LEWIS: The resident psychiatrist suspected alcoholism as a contributory factor to his condition. Traces of adolescent hookworm.

MOTOCAR: More distinguished than acne.

LEWIS: Malarial. Claimed army service in Flanders but could not prove it. Lost pay-book and discharge papers. Sapper with native troops was his description of the rank he attained.

MOTOCAR: Sapper with native troops. Sapper with native troops.

LEWIS: Discharged 3rd September 1928. Re-admitted 7th August 1934. Discharged. Re-admitted.

MOTOCAR: Discharged. Re-admitted.

LEWIS: Discharged. Re-admitted. Discharged. Re-admitted. After most of these entries it says voluntary. You understand that? He asked to come in, he asked to go out.

MOTOCAR: It was this man, my father, Senzangakona, who advised me to accept the offer to study abroad. Go, he said, learn to think, then write the true history of your people. I would rather die. I would rather die and be thrown into one of those ditches he dug.

LEWIS: 1953 was a bad year for him.

MOTOCAR: The Federation.

LEWIS: Fragmentation. Disorientation. Crisis of identity. Re-admitted. Discharged. Re-admitted. Discharged.

41

MOTOCAR: Ten years of it, ten years.

LEWIS: There appears to have been an alleviation of symptoms in 1964. He seemed far more optimistic.

MOTOCAR: The Federation collapsed. These was freedom all around him.

LEWIS: 1965 saw his worst breakdown yet. Paralysis. Loss of speech and motor power in one leg. Perpetual state of anxiety. Psychosurgery, November 15th.

MOTOCAR: U.D.I.

LEWIS: The operation was not a success. Schizophrenia advanced. Sense of inferiority. Acute depression. After several abortive courses of treatment he was sent to work at a farm near Inyanga, doing a job that was commensurate with his disability. He became a chicken-guard.

[*Pause*]

That is the last entry.

MOTOCAR: Will you give the file to Inspector Pickerill now? Put it in my bag with my stone, my books, my friends. He should have them all. Give him all the evidence he needs. I am guilty.

[*LEWIS gives PICKERILL the file. PICKERILL looks at it, then gets the briefcase and puts the file inside, then collects the books and stone.*]

MOTOCAR: I killed. We are always killing. I have heard it said that it is necessary. If so, then it is necessary to be mad. I found my limping, split-brain father and put him out of his misery. That is in the power of emperors. It is in the power of Jesuits. It is in the power of those who understand the truth of murder and the truth of emptiness, the truth of madness and the truth of necessity. Four truths, four Gospels, twelve Apostles, one hundred years, many numbers. Have you all your evidence, Inspector?

PICKERILL: I have.

MOTOCAR: And all your numbers? And all your words?

PICKERILL: I am trying.

MOTOCAR: I killed my father, Mr Sophocles. I put him down like an old dog who cannot see. Now I am going blind. He wanted to die as I do now, and take it all with him. We have no future in our family. That belongs to my friends on the switchboard. Hm, what names my father gave his children, what names we get given. Lobengula. Victoria. Mauch. Moffat. Moshesh. Mzilikazi. Monomotapa, Motocar...Who has heard of us? And who will ever listen but ourselves?

[*DONAHUE and SYMONDS have worked through all the shades of grey and are now holding a pitch-black sheet.*]

Now, don't fold that one away. That's my father's. I would like to have it for the journey.

[*DONAHUE puts the sheet over MOTOCAR's shoulders. He wraps it round, squats.*]
The door is being opened. We can all go through. Goodbye, Mr Sophocles, goodbye.
[*Slow fade to blackout.*]

Nkosi sikalele Afrika

BY ENOCH SONTONGA, ARRANGED BY STEPHEN BOXER

Unaccompanied

RICHARD III
PART TWO

For Clio

CHARACTERS

GEORGE ORWELL: born Eric Blair in India, 1903. Went to Eton, joined Burma Police, then became a writer. Fought for the Republican cause in the Spanish Civil War. His most popular books are *Animal Farm* (published 1945), and his last novel, *1984*, written in 1948. Died of tuberculosis in 1950.

RICHARD III: born 1452, Fotheringhay, last son of Richard, Duke of York, and Cicely Neville. After his brother's death (King Edward IV) in 1482, he was designated Protector. Crushing a conspiracy by Elizabeth Woodville (King Edward's widow) to seize power, he accepted the suggestion that the sons of his brother were bastards by reason of Edward's alleged first marriage to Eleanor Butler, and ascended the throne himself. His nephews (the Princes in the Tower) were placed in custody.

LOVELL, FRANK: born 1950, educated at Ampleforth and London School of Economics. Did postgraduate work in retail dynamics and ergo-selling at Massachusetts Institute of Technology before joining the United Nations as an adviser to the Commission on Entertainment Shortfalls in the Third World. Moved to the Ministry of Sport (Indoor Games Division) in 1983 as Sales Promotion Director. Awarded Queen's Commerce Medal. Hobbies: dialect poetry and country dancing.

LOVELL, FRANCIS: born circa 1450, educated with Richard at Middleham in Yorkshire by the Earl of Warwick. Became Richard's High Chamberlain and fought with him at Bosworth, but escaped, re-appearing at a later rebellion against Henry Tudor by Lambert Simnel posing as Prince Edward. Escaped again and disappeared. In 1708 a skeleton was discovered seated at a table with bread and wine, in a secret vault under Minster Lovell, his house.

McMASTERS, GEORGE: born 1951, educated at local grammar school and St. Andrews where he graduated in Business and Commerce Studies with International Relations as a subsidiary. Worked for Ford Motor Company, Dagenham and Detroit, then the International Leisure Council as Chairman of Card-Games Regulations Standardization Committee. Joined the Ministry of Sport (Indoor Games Division) in 1982 as Marketing Surveys Controller. Hobbies: gliding and the scouting movement.

McMASTERS, GEORGE: born 1451, Peniquick, near Edinburgh, of poor parents. Apprenticed to a merchant banker in Edinburgh and rose to become a partner. Made an alderman in the year before Richard III invaded Scotland and demanded the surrender of the city. As one of the principal negotiators he was considered responsible for the arrangement whereby the English King was allowed to enter Edinburgh unopposed. Unable to remain in the city after the withdrawal of the English army, he accompanied King Richard to London and became the chamberlain of Cicely, Duchess of York. Died in 1499 of jaundice.

ELIZABETH WOODVILLE: daughter of Earl Rivers and widow of Lord Ferrers, a Lancastrian supporter killed at Saint Albans, by whom she had two children. Married Edward IV secretly on May Day 1464 and bore him three children—Edward and Richard (the Princes in the Tower), and Elizabeth who later married Henry Tudor. After the marriage, Henry Tudor locked her away in a nunnery in Bermondsey. Died 1492.

EDWARD V (born 1470) and RICHARD, DUKE OF YORK (born 1474): the 'Princes in the Tower', sons of Edward IV and Elizabeth Woodville. Dates of death unknown.

CICELY, DUCHESS OF YORK: born 1414, Raby in County Durham, daughter of Ralph, Earl of Westmorland. Aunt of Warwick the Kingmaker. Had twelve children, only seven of whom survived infancy—Edmund (killed in battle), Edward IV, George, Duke of Clarence (executed for treason by Edward IV, his brother) and Richard III (killed at Bosworth) were her sons. After Richard's death she retired to her castle at Berkhamsted and lived as a religious recluse until her death in 1495.

CHRYSOSTOM, CHRISTOPHOLOUS: born circa 1146 in Constantinople, son of a Byzantine church craftsman. When the city was besieged by the Turks in 1450 the child was taken north to Dubrovnik where he was later apprenticed to the painter Mappani. After arguing with his master, switched to glass-making and travelled throughout Central Europe and then the Mediterranean, working in Milan for the Sforza, in Rimini for the Malatesta, and Florence for the Medici. Went to France and Burgundy in 1482-3 and arrived in England at the height of his international reputation. On his return to his home in Genoa he established a glass factory and built up a major industry which was transferred to Venice twenty years later by his natural son Georgio. Date of death unknown.

LOUISE PENHALYGON: born 1960, Penzance. Graduated from Exeter Technical College in Audio-Visual Aids in 1979 and joined the Imperial War Museum as a demonstrator of early gas equipment. Became Projects Co-ordinator Grade III at Ministry of Sport (Indoor Games Division) in 1983. Hobbies include ornithology and playing records.

The first performance of *Richard III Part Two* was given at the Traverse Theatre Club, Edinburgh on August 24th 1977 by Paines Plough, directed by Edward Adams. The cast was as follows:

GEORGE ORWELL RICHARD III }	Stephen Boxer
CICELY PRINCE EDWARD }	Harriet Walter
LOUISE PRINCE RICHARD }	Diana Kyle
McMASTERS	Robert McIntosh
LOVELL	Eric Richard
ELIZABETH WOODVILLE	Fiona Victory
CHRYSOSTOM	Joe Marcell

NOTES

The rôles shown as doubled in the original production are recommended as being played that way in any casting; but the rôles of PRINCE EDWARD/CICELY and LOUISE/RICHARD may be performed as separate parts. RICHARD III and GEORGE ORWELL *must* be doubled.

Two acting levels help with the flow of time-shifts in the play between 1948, 1984 and 1484. Scene changes are not recommended, except by using direction of dialogue, music and strategic moves. The play should flow between its locations.

Whenever possible McMASTERS and LOVELL should change from 1984 to 1484 costume and vice versa in order to identify the time they are working in, but this should not impede the action and may occasionally be dispensed with, once the convention has been established. As a general rule, LOUISE is not intended to make stage exits, but moves to and from the control areas.

A textile backdrop showing the Betrayal game board, (the design of which is left to the imagination of the director and designer), can be used as a cover for the stained-glass window, then drawn aside as curtains on the final scene.

The Death and Nativity cards should be large, simple and able to be produced from the main rostrum beneath the Betrayal board, either as flip-overs, or hinged panels. The plastic punch-cards out of the Betrayal box itself must be exact copies.

The chess-table, chairs, stools and other stage furniture used should have a heavy medieval feel and tone in order to contrast with the chrome dazzle of the electric piano. Two ultra modern chairs in chrome and plastic can be used for McMASTERS and LOVELL in a position, or on a level where 1984 action is predominant.

The music can be played by the acting company or an orchestra. Notes on the music are provided with the score at the end of the text.

Instruments used in the original production were: lute-guitar, rebec, Nordic lyre, psaltery, dulcimer, guitar, electric piano, glockenspiel, sopranino and tenor recorders, penny whistle, percussion.

Wherever possible, the instruments should be used as helpers and illustrators of the action, almost as secondary characters. They can be handled, tuned, knitted into the story to give the impression of RICHARD III being a man who loved music and surrounded himself with instruments as well as men.

ACT ONE

The Betrayal board background is revealed as the lights go swiftly up. GEORGE ORWELL, dressed in pyjamas and dressing-gown, stands in front of the board, a typescript in his hand. He places it on the chess-table. The chess-board is still set for a game which has been abandoned. Some of the pieces have been knocked over. Stage left is a control area where LOUISE is sitting. She wears a tee-shirt with 'Indoor Games' across the chest. All the instruments are stacked or placed here, also a tape-deck and amplification system. LOUISE remains in shadow, an electric piano keyboard in front of her.

ORWELL: My name is George Orwell and I have written a book, here. As a socialist all my life—too late to find another word for what I believe in—the book perturbs me. I don't feel at all easy about it. My agent thinks it will be misunderstood and fail. I'm afraid I got a little upset as that was a conclusion I had come to myself. I have set it in 1984—this being 1948. It is an arbitrary date but it is the future. So that means I am being prophetic, which is alarming in itself. This I do not attempt to excuse. We must have prophets, ask the government, and a dying one has always been conceded a certain status, indulged. [*Coughs*] I have TB, a contagious disease of the lungs passed on spittle. My book may drown in a flood of it. More than anything, I don't want this book of mine sensationalized in its more trivial aspects. After a decade of war against fascism—on which I have some opinions —my main theme needs to be politically clear. For example, I say that in 1984 the middle-class will adopt the uniform of the working-class and prance around in overalls; and that the new television-sets appearing everywhere will mean the end of private life by this time. Perhaps I am going too far. Could be. My argument that English socialism will be turned into a machine of oppression by successive gangs of university lecturers, technocrats, scientists and publicity men, all of rigorous middle-class background like myself, ah, that is what will be taken up. I will suffer for that. I will be accused of betraying the cause; and that will be painful. I will be accused of betraying my own past; and that will be agonizing. [*Coughs. Takes a handkerchief out of his pocket, covers his mouth, looks at it, grimaces, puts it back in his pocket.*] What I am deeply concerned about in *1984* is the wilful destruction of historical truth by over-powerful, self-righteous governments. Real history is a law, like gravity. There is no greater power in the human present than the human past. The present *is* the past. Winston Smith, the hero of my book —called after Churchill who wasn't averse to rewriting history himself, in imitation of Stalin we could say—Winston Smith works in the Ministry of Truth as an expert operator of Double-think. That's his job. Let me illustrate. [*Setting up the fallen chess-pieces one by one.*] Stage One—you make up a story for propaganda purposes. Stage Two—you deliberately believe that story yourself. Stage Three—you force yourself to forget that you created it. Stage Four—you accept it as history. So history is plastic. Its patterns are in a state of constant disturbance. [*Pause*] How did we get into this position? Why did we allow ourselves to become so arrogant as to think that we have the right to re-shape the past? These were lives people led, they happened, happened in their terms, not ours. History belongs to the people who lived it first! They have a right to be heard, always. [*Pause*] But ought I to post this book to my publishers? My enemies will do everything in their power to discredit me for having written it. They will give me no peace.

[*ORWELL exits, taking the typescript.*
General lighting up. LOUISE takes up a microphone, flicks a switch on the console.]

LOUISE: [*Over loudspeakers.*] This is the final call for delegates to the Ministry of Sport Indoor Games Division Conference for sales executives and operatives to go to the Danube Room. Will all delegates please go to the Danube Room where the conference is about to begin.

[*LOUISE switches off the amplification system. LOVELL and McMASTERS enter in smart, clean pressed overalls which look tailor-made, carrying two game boxes. The top one reads 'Big Brother'.*]

McMASTERS: Introductions are hardly necessary, but this is Louise Penhalygon, Projects Co-ordinator...

LOUISE: Hello.

McMASTERS: Frank Lovell, Sales Promotion Director, Indoor...

LOVELL: Hello.

McMASTERS: And I'm George McMasters, Marketing Surveys Controller, Indoor. Now, if any one of you is worried about this conference, forget it. 1984 has been a record year for the Indoor Games Division, thanks to you, the best sales team I ever worked with. You're terrific, every single one of you.

[*McMASTERS puts the game boxes down, the lid of one still hidden.*]

LOVELL: 1984 has been a marvellous year, marvellous. Our George Orwell promotion has been a fantastic success. The Big Brother unit became the top-selling board-game in the Common Market—

909,771, plus an export figure to trade areas outside the EEC of 801,567. Phenomenal. We never imagined Orwell's ideas had such pull.

McMASTERS: But this coming year, 1985, has got to be even better. New targets have been set and we have to hit them. It really is export or die. Now Orwell's comic novel is well-known, all those jokes, Big Brother, Newspeak, Doublethink, they've been enjoyed for thirty years. But he is nothing beside the figure at the centre of our new project.

[*LOUISE plays a chord on the electric piano.*]

LOVELL: He's notorious!

[*Another chord, building.*]

McMASTERS: Our greatest villain!

[*Another chord, building.*]

LOVELL: A political monster!

[*Another chord.*]

McMASTERS: The archetype of all cold-hearted killers!

[*Final swelling chord.*]

McMASTERS }
LOVELL   } Richard the Third!

McMASTERS: The game? Betrayal! [*Shows the lid of the box.*]

LOVELL: It will be a world-beater.

McMASTERS: Monopoly, look out. Diplomacy, forget it.

[*LOUISE changes to softer, more reflective music, LOVELL speaks over.*]

LOVELL: So at the heart of the game, there's a man, and a mystery? Was he guilty? Did he murder so many?

McMASTERS: Henry the Sixth's son, Henry the Sixth, his own brother Clarence...and the Princes in the Tower? There's a tale that touches everyone. The boys. The boys. Did he kill the boys? And if he did...why? Tantalizing stuff. [*Opens the game.*]

LOVELL: All we know is that they disappeared, and no one ever admitted that they were dead. So, our game takes place in the right environment—speculation! You play Betrayal on Monday —he did. You play Betrayal on Tuesday—he didn't. That's the kind of zesty, quicksilver fun we can offer. I tell you, we're on to a winner!

[*Music fades out. Enter ELIZABETH WOODVILLE.*]

McMASTERS: Pieces. Let's have a look at the pieces. Once again our backroom boys have done us proud. Look at this. Have you ever seen such detail? Such finish? And the style is exact. Real quality.

LOVELL: Elizabeth Woodville, widow of King Edward, mother of the Princes.

[*Enter PRINCE EDWARD and PRINCE RICHARD.*]

McMASTERS: And here are the boys. The tall one is Edward, the

53

uncrowned King, shoved aside by his uncle on his way to the throne. The short one is Richard, Duke of York. Look at that. Beautiful craftmanship. See the way they glide across the board.

ELIZABETH: Come and play chess until your Uncle Richard arrives. That will pass the time.

PRINCE EDWARD: Mother, no more games, please. That's all we've done since father died, play games.

PRINCE RICHARD: Why don't you do something to get us out of here?

ELIZABETH: I will, I will. Don't forget I've been virtually under house-arrest myself for the last year. I'm working on getting you free, you must trust me. Now, chess. A game will keep you occupied. But when you hear Uncle Richard coming I want you straight back upstairs so we can all come down together and face him as a family...

PRINCE EDWARD: I don't want to see him. I hate his guts.

PRINCE RICHARD: So do I.

ELIZABETH: You will do as you're told. I want you both to be on your best behaviour. Give your uncle no cause to criticize you. If you do, you could spoil everything. Sit down at the table. Edward, you take the black, Richard, the white.

PRINCE RICHARD: I had white last time. I want the black.

PRINCE EDWARD: Don't be so stupid, as if it mattered. Come on then.

ELIZABETH: You know how to play?

PRINCE EDWARD: Vaguely. Mother, we're really sick of amusing ourselves. We want you to *do* something! Uncle Richard will never let us go...

ELIZABETH: This is the king. This is the queen. This is the bishop, knight, castle. These are the pawns. Checkmate means the king is dead.

PRINCE EDWARD: I'd kill him if I had the chance.

PRINCE RICHARD: Mother, if there's kings and queens and bishops and knights on the board, why aren't there princes?

ELIZABETH: You should know why. They're all locked up in the castles.

[*ELIZABETH exits.*]

LOVELL: See what I mean? We're offering so much. We can really break through into the big time with Betrayal. 1985 is the five hundredth anniversary of the Battle of Bosworth at which Richard the Third was killed. Remember Bosworth. Important. Significant. The end.

McMASTERS: The final square. The pay-off.

LOVELL: Betrayal—teeming with these marvellous medieval characters—kicks off on Christmas Eve 1484 at Berkhamsted Castle, gallops excitingly through winter, spring and summer and ends in August, the day of reckoning.

[*PRINCE EDWARD and PRINCE RICHARD start to play chess.*]

McMASTERS: Hear him coming? Over the hill, down the lane. A cold, cold day but you can see quite clearly. The King is coming.

LOVELL: Into the courtyard, off his horse, up the steps, through the door, into the corridor...this is the game, and this is the man!

RICHARD: [*Off*] Hello! Anyone at home? I'm here!

[*PRINCE EDWARD and PRINCE RICHARD sweep the chess pieces away into a bag and run off, terrified. Enter RICHARD III in a long cloak, bent over, hunchbacked.*]

Where is everyone? Rouse yourselves! The King is here! God, it's cold. Where are you all? [*Whisks off his cloak to reveal a mandolin on his back. He takes it off.*] Come on down! Let me see you!

[*McMASTERS and LOVELL put on medieval surcoats which cover the tops of their overalls.*]

LOVELL: Sire.

McMASTERS: Sire.

RICHARD: There you are. No, no, up, up. No formalities. Where have you been hiding? Come here. [*Embraces them.*] How are my old friends? Steady as ever. Let me look at you both. Never was a king so fortunate in his friends. I've missed you both.

McMASTERS: Welcome to Berkhamsted, sire. We've been waiting for you.

LOVELL: Hello, Richard. You've made good time.

RICHARD: Where's my mother?

McMASTERS: She's in the middle of a lecture given by a wandering friar on the practical uses of self-denial. She'll cut the household budget and then tell us to blame it on God.

RICHARD: Is she well, in herself?

McMASTERS: Stronger than ever. I don't know how she does it.

RICHARD: Go and tell her I'm here and that I'd like to see her.

[*McMASTERS exits.*]

Has Elizabeth arrived yet?

LOVELL: She has.

RICHARD: I expect you were pleased to see her.

LOVELL: As a drowning man delights in water.

RICHARD: I'm sure she has her good points.

LOVELL: Maybe, but I'm not risking my life looking for them.

RICHARD: Bear with her for my sake. I need her here. I'll explain later.

[*Enter McMASTERS with a robe for RICHARD.*]

McMASTERS: Your mother has a few prayers to finish, then she'll be with you. God is in a chatty mood today.

[*Enter ELIZABETH with PRINCE EDWARD and PRINCE RICHARD. PRINCE EDWARD is coughing.*]

ELIZABETH: There you are Richard, at last. The boys and I have been listening for your horse.

RICHARD: He's a quiet walker. Hello Elizabeth. [*Kisses her.*] And what's this, Edward?

PRINCE EDWARD: I have to stay in bed.

PRINCE RICHARD: He's very ill. He coughs so much he keeps me awake at nights.

RICHARD: That is worrying. Is their bedchamber warm and dry, Frank?

LOVELL: The best in the house.

RICHARD: And you Richard, how is your voice? As pure as ever? I hope you will sing for me later. I boast about the voices of my nephews.

ELIZABETH: He will be glad to. I think Edward should go back to bed now, with your permission.

RICHARD: Edward, we will cure this cough. Use your mind, your will-power. Think to yourself—this cough does not exist. Believe it, and the cough will go away. Go on, say it. This cough does not exist.

PRINCE EDWARD: This cough does not exist. [*Coughs*] I knew it wouldn't work.

PRINCE RICHARD: He doesn't know what he is talking about.

ELIZABETH: Richard, don't be insolent.

PRINCE EDWARD: I'm not a bastard!

PRINCE RICHARD: Neither am I!

PRINCE EDWARD: My father was king. I should be king...

ELIZABETH: Edward, stop it!

PRINCE RICHARD: And if he's not king, I should be. I'm next.

ELIZABETH: Get upstairs this minute...

RICHARD: No, no, let them go on. Anything else you want to say to me? You might as well get it all off your chest. No?

LOVELL: They want a good thrashing, the pair of them!

RICHARD: Quiet, Frank.

ELIZABETH: I'm sorry, Richard. They have behaved disgracefully...

PRINCE EDWARD: We're sorry too, aren't we?

PRINCE RICHARD: Yes, to the bottom of our hearts.

PRINCE EDWARD: We learnt something for you, Uncle.

PRINCE RICHARD: It's not much, but we worked hard at it. I'm ready.

PRINCE EDWARD } The Cat, the Rat, and Lovell our dog,
PRINCE RICHARD } Rule all England under an hog.

LOVELL: I'll break your bloody necks!

[*PRINCE EDWARD and PRINCE RICHARD run off. RICHARD stops LOVELL following them.*]

RICHARD: Leave them, Frank. They are only children. Thank you for the entertainment, Elizabeth.

ELIZABETH: It had nothing to do with me. If my sons pick things up out of the gutter it is not my fault. It is you who has charge of their education. But I will, with your permission, go and see to it that we have no more embarrassing outbursts. May I?

RICHARD: Of course.

[*ELIZABETH exits.*]

LOVELL: Some chance you've got of having a peaceful Christmas with her around. She'd cause a riot in a graveyard.

McMASTERS: She put the boys up to it. They'd never dare talk to you like that without her support. That was all carefully rehearsed.

RICHARD: Quite likely. But she is my brother's widow, and my present policy is to contain her mischief, and her sons, and let her live. [*Pause*] Now, this is to go no further at this time, but news has come from agents in France that Henry Tudor plans to invade England next summer and seize the throne.

LOVELL: God's teeth! As soon as that? We're not ready for them.

McMASTERS: With what army? What money?

RICHARD: French army, French money. And some help from friends at home. [*Pause*] You see why I wanted her here?

McMASTERS: Dame Elizabeth?

LOVELL: Who else?

[*Enter CICELY, Duchess of York, unseen.*]

RICHARD: Tudor is negotiating to marry her daughter. If he is successful his plan is to unite York, the lady, with Lancaster, himself, and bring the realm together. Only the boys stand in his way. They are Elizabeth's bargaining factor.

LOVELL: Jesus Christ. That woman would haggle over how many pennies to put on a dead man's eyes.

CICELY: Kill her. Hello my son. Did you have a good journey? Yes, kill her. God understands acts of political necessity, he must do, otherwise the world would have fallen to pieces years ago.

RICHARD: Mother...

CICELY: The woman is not to be trusted. You've got thinner and you look tired. Why are you so kind to her? 'To deliver thee from the strange woman, even from the stranger who flattereth with her words.' Proverbs, chapter two, verse sixteen...

McMASTERS: [*In unison*] Proverbs, chapter two, verse sixteen...

CICELY: I would have no hesitation in disposing of the bitch. I am sorry if my castle is cold but it has been empty for months. Kiss me. We have been very busy preparing for you. This, I said, must be his best Christmas.

[*Enter ELIZABETH holding up a handkerchief spotted with blood.*]

ELIZABETH: Look, Edward has coughed blood. [*Pause*] I'm not saying that it's anyone's fault but blood is blood. That is very worrying. [*Pause*] Oh let us not enter into any debate on the subject. Brr, there's a draught from somewhere...

[*Enter CHRYSOSTOM, a magnificently dressed negro wearing an enormous Renaissance hat and carrying a jewelled bag and a long whitewashed board. They recoil.*]

CHRYSOSTOM: [*Chuckling*] Hello. It's very cold out there. [*He takes off his hat and executes a phenomenally contrived bow.*] That's how they do it in Burgundy these days. Silly isn't it?

LOVELL: Hold it right there!

CHRYSOSTOM: Harmless, harmless. A wanderer. I am expected.

McMASTERS: Identify yourself! This is a royal household!

CHRYSOSTOM: From Byzantium. My father was in mosaics, I am in glass. A chip off the old rock.

LOVELL: How did you get here?

CHRYSOSTOM: I am the result of a clandestine cultural exchange between Africa and Asia Minor.

McMASTERS: Right, you stay where you are. Don't move. Drop everything. Keep absolutely still. Put your hands where I can see them.

[*Pause. CHRYSOSTOM is searched, his bags examined during the next sequence. RICHARD watches him, wary.*]

LOVELL: [*Picking up the board*] What's this?

CHRYSOSTOM: I could be a fakir.

McMASTERS: Say that again, slowly.

CHRYSOSTOM: A fakir. An Indian comedian. They induce mirth in their audiences by lying on a bed of nails. As you can see, I have come strongly under the influence of western civilization. I have had all the nails pulled out. No, not at all. I never even bothered to put them in. [*Pause*] This is my sketching board, for my designs. Have you finished fondling me?

LOVELL: Sire, I don't like the look of this character...

CHRYSOSTOM: Tomorrow I'll try harder. I've only changed my codpiece twice today and I have a huge selection of ridiculous hats.

RICHARD: What are you doing here?

CHRYSOSTOM: I have an invitation to spend Christmas here from the King's mother. [*To ELIZABETH.*] Here I am and thank you for asking me. I have kept a careful list of my expenses so far... we can take my home base as Genoa for the moment, but I think we'll have to keep the fee open for negotiation as the exchange rate for rose nobles has been dropping against all the major European currencies as a result of your persistent political unrest...

ELIZABETH: I am not the King's mother.

CICELY: That is me. You must be the craftsman I ordered.

CHRYSOSTOM: Rather the executive you asked for.

CICELY: Have you the mystery of making coloured windows?

58

CHRYSOSTOM: I possess it.

CICELY: This man is here at my invitation. His name is Chrysostom.

CHRYSOSTOM: Call me Chris. [*Looking at RICHARD.*] Is this the subject?

RICHARD: This is the King.

CHRYSOSTOM: I see a lot of kings but few men. [*Looks at the window.*]

CICELY: I did not think you would be black.

CHRYSOSTOM: Neither did my father.

RICHARD: Mother, I want this to be a family Christmas...no business.

CICELY: Richard, you are the last of my sons, the last of my men. You came to me late in life and you were the smallest, and the weakest, needing most from me. So, I love you best of all my children, and now you are King of the English. When you die I want there to be something beautiful, something timeless to keep you in the public mind. I will pay for it.

CHRYSOSTOM: You want a timeless window? Timeless comes expensive.

CICELY: Isn't that the quality of great art?

CHRYSOSTOM: One shared with great lies. But you're the customer and you are gifted with unfailing, relentless rectitude.

CICELY: Will you agree, Richard? He has a fine reputation.

RICHARD: What for? His tailor?

CHRYSOSTOM: [*Bowing again*] Sire, it is a pleasure for the world's best stained glass window maker to meet the world's most blood-stained widow maker.
[*Pause*]

RICHARD: You believe all you hear?

CHRYSOSTOM: If one circulates, one lives with rumour.

RICHARD: Mother, I will have to be persuaded. This creature has no natural part in a Christian festival.

CHRYSOSTOM: King, what am I selling? What can I do for you? Why should your mother pay me for something so fragile, so insubstantial as a stained glass window? I'll tell you. You need a new image.

LOVELL: That's what we've been telling him.

CHRYSOSTOM: You've got to change the way that people think of you.

McMASTERS: When you say 'Richard the Third' to anyone, pow! I want to see their eyes light up and their hands head straight for their wallets!

CHRYSOSTOM: The Good Prince must have a good image. He's got to concentrate on that, keep in the public eye, shape what is known, disguise that which might confuse, cover up that which is unsightly.

59

LOVELL: Be practical...

McMASTERS: Cultivate the right approach...

CHRYSOSTOM: Well, the way I look at it is this—image-making is a
    whole new business when you see it in relation to politics. It
    suddenly has power, importance. Up until now the industry has
    been crude, rudimentary—look at the work of your English
    portrait painters, it's laughable, useless—it hasn't been adapted to
    your needs.

ELIZABETH: You're preparing to idealize him. Is that what you
    want, mother-in-law?

CICELY: You balance extremes with extremes. Let him do it,
    Richard.

RICHARD: One window? What will one window achieve. Will all the
    people of England come to Berkhamsted to see it?

CHRYSOSTOM: Copies, facsimiles, hand-outs, brochures, leaflets...

LOVELL: Posters, medals, coins, clothes, badges...

McMASTERS: Shields, flags, buttons...*I can see it!*

LOVELL: *So can I!*

McMASTERS: You'll make a fortune!

CHRYSOSTOM: So will I.

RICHARD: In the face of such universal enthusiasm I can only say
    —go ahead.

LOVELL: Go ahead. May I speak to Mr Caxton?

McMASTERS: Caxton speaking. What can I do for you?

LOVELL: Big order coming your way. By appointment to the King.

CHRYSOSTOM: Tell him not to forget my commission.

McMASTERS: What do you want? Two-tone litho? Silk-screen? How
    many thousand? How many million? How many copies from the
    original?

ALL: [*Sing*]
    Reproductions, reproductions, let the image be widespread,
    reproductions, reproductions, the species never dead,
    introducing William Caxton with his hug and squeeze and press,
    introducing William Caxton who can multiply a yes
    or a no or a quick quick slow,
    or a sigh or a thought or a battle fought,
    or a prayer or a note from the deepest throat,
    or a love or a lie or a don't say die.

    Reproductions, reproductions, circulation, outlets, sales,
    reproductions, reproductions, this system never fails,
    introducing William Caxton with his comma, O and stop,
    introducing William Caxton who is getting to the top
    of the bottom, see the I's, you dot 'em,
    give the Q little tail, alphabetical snail
    give the J bloody hook for a judge's book
    have the B with a breast you'll find that sells best.

60

Reproductions, reproductions, get the screw down on the plate,
reproductions, reproductions, the lady's period is late,
introducing William Caxton with his black, prophetic hands,
introducing William Caxton who gave reproduction glands
and an organ, conclusion foregone,
success, hit the heights with your name in lights,
tell the world, here's the truth, grab a nation's youth,
do a run, thousands come and the campaign's won.

LOVELL: It's the answer, sire. This way you can change the situation instead of allowing the situation to change you.

RICHARD: Leave us alone. I would like a private word with this peacock.

[*McMASTERS, LOVELL, CICELY, ELIZABETH exit.*]

I let it pass at the time, but are the insults necessary for your art? Does it pay to be so provocative?

CHRYSOSTOM: Europe is full of gossip about you. Is it true that you have had the sons of King Edward murdered in the Tower of London?

RICHARD: [*Pause*] You will see them here, with your own eyes. That apart, watch your tongue.

CHRYSOSTOM: My apologies.

RICHARD: So, they talk about me?

CHRYSOSTOM: You are a man who...attracts much speculation.

RICHARD: Henry Tudor knows how to broadcast lies. In that he is more skilled than I. As for battle, that is another matter.

CHRYSOSTOM: They say he has a good chance against you.

RICHARD: He has never fought in his life, except from well to the rear. Tudor is a coward.

CHRYSOSTOM: Sire, all Europe's monarchs exhibit their military prowess from a safe distance nowadays. It is the new style. I have seen them, at ease, surrounded by maps, messages...having refreshments, drunk, with women...

RICHARD: That is a fashion we will not adopt here.

CHRYSOSTOM: It seems to make kings live longer.

RICHARD: As what? [*Pause*] A king leads. If he creates a risk, then he must share it. These are not kings you are talking about. They are desk-clerks.

CHRYSOSTOM: The window. May I have a free hand?

RICHARD: It is your mind my mother is paying for, not mine.

CHRYSOSTOM: One idea has just occurred to me during our discussion. We might think about introducing this motif. [*Shows RICHARD a skull design.*] I have used it a lot recently. There has been plague in Paris and Milan. It has been a good seller, very popular. We might find a place for it in our design.

[Dances and sings.]

> Sir, Emperor, Lord of all the ground,
> High Prince, son of a noble house,
> you must give up your golden apple,
> your blade-sceptre, treasure-trove,
> and with all dance my way,
> holding hands with Adam's children as they go,
> some going quick, some going slow.

> People look on this shell,
> the gestures in an antique dance,
> see what you are and where your nature leads,
> food for worms, uninstated trash with only words,
> and dead sons for remembrance.

> Here he sits who is a King,
> a live but dead, a doomed, inanimated thing.

> I have never learnt to dance with hope,
> but only at the mass with savage steps,
> who is the hardest is the most wise,
> the King would be better with the dancer's eyes.

[CICELY, LOVELL and McMASTERS re-enter.
During the dance, which should be in the spirit of the danse
macabre, LOVELL reveals a large card showing a skull (based
on CHRYSOSTOM's design which has been seen by RICHARD).
CICELY kneels down at the end of the dance. LOVELL and
McMASTERS take off their medieval surcoats and revert to their
1984 costume. McMASTERS takes a plastic punch-card out of
the Betrayal box. It is the skull design again, perforated.
RICHARD and CHRYSOSTOM withdraw.]

CICELY: I confess to Almighty God...

McMASTERS: This is the new design for the joker in the Chance
pack...

CICELY: ...that I have sinned exceedingly in thought, word and
deed...

LOVELL: When a player gets this joker he keeps it and when he finds
himself disabled or out of the game through forfeits, landing on
a penalty square, falling into a trap, then he plays this card and
it gets him going again...

CICELY: ...through my fault, through my fault, through my most
grievous fault...

McMASTERS: If the player finds himself in a one-to-one situation
then he can use the card and take a gamble by inserting it into
the game computer. Each card is punched up to provide a
different solution...see here...the eyes...the teeth...the player
might win, the player might lose...it's a last ditch ploy. You only

62

use it if you think the odds are stacked against you...what the computer prints out, that's fate...

CICELY: I confess to adultery. I confess to pride. I confess to keeping my mouth shut.

[*McMASTERS turns over another card which has a picture of an infant, smiling.*]

McMASTERS: In contrast...the Nativity Card. [*Shows punch-card of same design.*]

LOVELL: Each of the fifty noble family Dynasty Sets—all players must accumulate at least five by the inter-marriage share-out by the banker—must wait for a Nativity Card before they can start to plot for the throne and actually get on the board...

CICELY: I allowed the offspring of a common soldier to sit upon the throne of England, knowing the law that the illegitimate cannot inherit. Edward, as should have been seen from his tastes, was not his father's son. He was a bastard, Lord, as you know. [*Pause*] But I let him be king. What brings low the House of York will be my sin. I have sent to the Pope for a full pardon with goods and money. Upon my death I need the document tied around my neck with ribbon and buried with me.

LOVELL: By placing the Baby in the game computer the player opens out a whole new permutation which can lead, with luck and some skilful manipulation of resources, to the ultimate objective...first-born to throne.

McMASTERS: I can't stress enough the importance of these two cards—our friend old Hollow-Eyes, and Smiler here. They activate the game. Without them a player is hamstrung, useless. Be sure to point that out to all retailers, all demonstrators...watch out for the child and the bones...

[*LOVELL offers CICELY a crucifix which hangs round his neck. She kisses it, gets up. LOVELL and McMASTERS put their surcoats back on. RICHARD and CHRYSOSTOM come forward.*]

CICELY: Now, we'll leave you to come up with some good ideas. Is there anything else you need?

CHRYSOSTOM: No, thank you. If I may just...be around, part of the group, take a few notes, sketch...that will be fine.

CICELY: Good. Now, Richard, we would like some of your time. A quick word.

RICHARD: Mother, no state business...

CICELY: We sympathize with you about the death of your son, all of us. It was a bitter blow. But it is not the end of the world, not the world you live in. You must shake it off, come to terms with it.

LOVELL: It's the luck of the draw, some children never make it...

RICHARD: Shut up, Frank.

LOVELL: Yes, sire.

CICELY: You cannot afford to grieve so long. Strength is what matters. Show you're strong. Control it...

RICHARD: Have you finished?

CICELY: It's for your own good.

RICHARD: The matter is closed.

CICELY: I will not have the death of one boy responsible for the decline of this kingdom! You have the hammer and the anvil to make more children, make them...but you have one kingdom, one time, one life...one responsibility. To succeed. Be a great king, a memorable king, a king who will be part of the future...on his own terms. You determine how people think, you regulate what people do, you interpret life for them, you...

RICHARD: Mother...

CICELY: Let me finish.

RICHARD: I need time to get over my boy's death. It is cruel not to give me time.

CICELY: There is no time. You are losing your grip. You are playing into your enemies' hands. While you grieve, they congregate: while you mourn, they multiply.

   [*Pause*]

RICHARD: You feel this way, Frank? George?

McMASTERS: Yes, it's gone too far.

LOVELL: Right.

RICHARD: And you kept it to yourselves?

LOVELL: Until now. As your oldest friend I respected your grief, but now we must put that aside and think of the future. We must plan, get ready...

RICHARD: There was no better child, so good, so content, so advanced for his age. He could read by the time he was three. He could write by the time he was four. He could sing from written notes in his fifth year. A child for a new age. A child for a new time.

LOVELL: Richard, the boy is dead!

RICHARD: What a king he would have been.

CICELY: Then the father must do what the child intended. Think of your son inside yourself. There he lives. That is his future. What better way to keep him alive.

RICHARD: Mother, don't you understand? I was never worthy of him. I could not live up to my own child.

   [*Enter ELIZABETH and PRINCE RICHARD.*]

CICELY: That is an emotional nonsense. He was unformed, a jelly yet, far from manhood. What do you know about him? Dreams, hopes, perhaps some truth in them, but all of it guesswork. But look at you—experienced, strong, full-grown. As far as fitness for power is concerned there is no comparison. Child means incompetent, Richard. Child means unready.

ELIZABETH: Child means threat. Child means needle.

PRINCE RICHARD: [*Sings*]
>   Child means a man without beard or voice,
>   Child means a man without mortal fears.

ELIZABETH: [*Sings*]
>   Child means a woman who will rejoice,
>   Child means a woman in labour's tears.

CICELY: [*Sings*]
>   Don't admire the unlit fire, the absent flame,
>   The player who is not yet ready for the game.
>   Save your respect, try to protect the ideal of adult,
>   And when you find the perfect power, exult, exult!

RICHARD: [*Sings*]
>   Child is the me of yesterday,
>   Child is the person who haunts my bones.

ELIZABETH: [*Sings*]
>   Child is the bird in the month of May,
>   Child is the nightmare's moans and groans.

CICELY: [*Sings*]
>   You will find the human mind improves with age,
>   Abjuring excess, random rage,
>   Petulance, the baby's dance, the tantrum in the dark,
>   Preferring calculation, making mark.

PRINCE RICHARD, ELIZABETH, CICELY, RICHARD: [*Sing*]
>   Child means an argument in age,
>   Child means a feat of memory,
>   Child means a bird in a human cage,
>   Child means a knowledge of history,
>   Child means a man who is all regret,
>   Child means a woman with fading looks,
>   Child means that life is not over yet,
>   Child means a marker within thy books.

[*Lights change. TV chimes played by LOUISE.*]

ELIZABETH: This is a party political broadcast on behalf of the Tudors. Richard the Third was in his mother's womb for two years and when he was born he had hair down to his waist and a full set of teeth. His first conscious act was to bite clean through the nipple of his wet-nurse. This ugly, vicious infant was deformed—a withered hand, club foot, crooked back. Turning him over in his cradle was a physiological nightmare. Undersized, weak and sickly, he managed to stagger through his early years to boyhood. At the age of eight he was further pushed towards pathological abnormality when his father and brother Edmund were decapitated by the genial, fun-loving forces of Margaret of Anjou. From that moment on this abortive, paranoid personality became obsessed with murder and unnatural crime. At number

11 Downing Street the Chancellor, Sir Thomas More, described
him as a symbol of evil rather than flesh and blood while
William Shakespeare reports in the Globe today that he actually
overheard the leader of the Plantagenet party say 'I am deter-
mined to prove a villain and hate the idle pleasure of these days.'
[*TV chimes out. Lights change back.*]

RICHARD: The lies that Tudor spreads about me!

LOVELL: Henry Tudor does what he must. He says, I'm out to win.
I'll do what I can, do what needs to be done. Frenchmen,
Germans, he doesn't care. He's a very practical man. Don't under-
estimate him, it will do you no credit.

RICHARD: He is preferred to me. I have improved the law, reduced
taxation, protected our towns, been as fair as I can. But this man
is preferred to me. I say a king has to earn his place. What has he
done?

CICELY: He has put up his sign and opened his shop. That is all.

RICHARD: You trust people, they let you down. You give them gifts,
they throw them in your face. You hold out a hand of friend-
ship, they break your fingers. Why? Why?

CHRYSOSTOM: [*Sings*]
No one knows but de Lord
why dis suffering is so,
but one thing dat we know,
suffering is here to stay.

ALL: [*Sing*]   Yeh, yeh, yeh, yeh,
dat much is reliable in life

CICELY: [*Sings*]
No one knows but de Lord

ALL: [*Sing*]   no one knows but de Lord
no one knows but de Lord
but what does de Lord know?

He knows man born to die,   } *Chorus*
he knows man born to die,
he knows man born to die,
dat aint much to leave us with.

RICHARD: [*Sings*]
Lord now take Thou my troubles
and sort them out for me,

ALL: [*Sing*]   And sort them out for him!

RICHARD: [*Sings*]
for I have only a short time here
and Thou hast eternity.

66

ALL: [*Sing*]   Thou hast eternity!
No one knows but de Lord,
no one knows but de Lord,
no one knows but de Lord,
but what does de Lord know?

         He knows man born to die,
he knows man born to die,
he knows man born to die,
dat aint much to leave us with.

Chorus

RICHARD: [*Sings*]
    I just wanna live in peace, Lord
just like an ordinary man,

ALL: [*Sing*]   Just like an ordinary man!

RICHARD: [*Sings*]
    I wanna eat and sleep and laugh, Lord,
please help me if you can.

ALL: [*Sing*]   Please help him if you can.

   [*Repeat chorus.*]

CHRYSOSTOM: Now the Lord, he says, tell me some of the troubles you've seen. Give me a list of the lies, give me a boxful of betrayals. I can take it, says the Lord.

ALL: [*Sing*]   He can take it, says the Lord,
he can take it, says the Lord,
that aint much to leave us with.

CICELY: [*Sings*]
    Oh he saw his Daddy cut down
and crowned with a paper crown!

RICHARD: [*Sings*]
    They murdered a brother of mine
and drowned another in wine.

ELIZABETH: [*Sings*]
    He killed off my brother and son,
that's how his kingdom was won.

CHRYSOSTOM: The Lord has heard, and now he says, Richard, boy, turn the mind from governing the land and have a try at ruling of the people. Stop being so organic and symbolic and integrated with the nuts of nature. Forget the farmyard, yea! Forget the bull, forget the fox, forget the hog. Be-e-e rational, and national, be sane, be Greek baby, be re-born!

RICHARD: [*Sings*]

> Peace is Man's richest possession,
> and leads him home to Heaven,
> peace of soul, peace of mind,
> peace from plague, peace from war.
>
> There's wisdom in what you say,
> advice not to be forgotten,
> the choice is mine,
> an old and trusted, or a new line.

[*Scream off. Enter PRINCE RICHARD running to ELIZABETH. She catches him in her arms. LOVELL and McMASTERS start taking off their surcoats.*]

PRINCE RICHARD: I think my brother Edward is dead!

[*Pause. LOVELL covers the Nativity Card with the Death Card.*]

ELIZABETH: Richard, I would like a word with you...

LOVELL: [*Sings*]

> Now, these are the rules of the game,
> all players get treated the same,
> no player can use his own dice,
> no virtue can choose its own vice.

ALL: [*Sing*]

> Now, these are the rules of the game,
> all players get treated the same,
> no player can use his own dice,
> no virtue can choose its own vice.
>
> All players are given a chance,
> you can act, you can sing, you can dance,
> you can breed, you can die, you can steal,
> you can freeze, you can fry, you can deal.
>
> [*Dance*]
> On your way, Fotheringhay,
> good throw, Ludlow,
> three and carry, Canterbury,
> a go you lose, back to Bruges,
> fiddle 'em, Middleham,
> balk at York,
> take a Chance card and then advance to Carmarthen,
> darn it, Barnet,
> try again, Amiens,
> you seem to be heading for a show-down at Edinburgh,
> tilt of the board, Stony Stratford,
> lucky man, Nottingham,
> in the red, Berkhamsted,
> what you worth, Bosworth.

Now these are the rules of the game,
shake the dice when I call out your name,
throw a three or a four and a five,
and we'll see who is staying alive.

[General exit. Lights fade to blackout.]

ACT TWO

Enter characters to instruments. The 'Peace' theme is played as the lights brighten. Enter ORWELL in an overcoat and muffler, carrying a parcel. Music fades. LOVELL and McMASTERS are in 1484 surcoats.

ORWELL: I feel guilty about *1984*, as if it were a trick. But it's not. Nor is it a stab in the back. [*Coughs, brings the bloody handkerchief out of his pocket.*] As perhaps my last book—you want to try writing and coughing as a routine rhythm—I would have liked to give it a more hopeful, idealistic note, less pessimistic, paranoid even. Can I do that with the way English socialism is going? When it happens, and this is the tragedy, people will not realize. It will have grown round them, become familiar. Continuous war, continuous conflict, state of emergency, backs to the wall, a relentless crisis day in day out...so you must do this, you must do that. Very easy. The screen, the man who asks all the questions for you, then answers them—who is he but your friend? Your brother? [*Coughs*] I say that now, this year, history has to be made sacred. Our past must be preserved *as it was*! The socialism we are growing into invites us all to be children, and me a dying man. Am I going to suck a dummy on my death-bed? Well, it's ready to go off. It will get bad reviews, oh yes. Orwell has followed the classical pattern: revolutionary, radical, revisionist, reactionary, cradle to grave, Labour to Conservative. My old friends will call me all the names under the sun. [*Coughs*] What else can I do with my experience? Ignore it? Shall I go to the Post Office? I honestly don't want to. I care about how I will be remembered and I'd rather it was for my honesty and my support of the working-class than for my books. But it's written. I wrote it, fully aware of what I was doing. *1984* was inside me. [*Coughs*] A stamp, the red box, a slow walk back. That is the immediate future. I hate this book and all it stands for. [*Exits*]

ELIZABETH: [*Coming forward*] My big brother Anthony was a writer. He was the author of the first book printed on William Caxton's new printing-press. He had enjoyed a wide experience of life and travelled beyond the Alps in search of the Holy Grail, and as diplomat for my husband, King Edward. While he was in Florence at the court of the Medici in the late sixties, he was at the house of a lawyer having dinner. Upstairs, the lawyer's wife was being delivered of a baby. At the point when the physician went to cut the umbilical cord, the child shouted out, very loudly, 'Affila quel coltello', 'sharpen that knife'. Later, my brother saw the child and heard it christened with the Devil's name of Nicholas. Then he left the house and never saw the Machiavelli family again, but always remembered them with fear and wonder.

McMASTERS: [*Sings*]

> The earth will not be the centre,
> philosophers will torment her:
> Life's wheel will turn on an axis
> of good commercial practice:
> read, write old Greek, new Italian,
> file God's head off your medallion,
> scratch Man's head there,
> based on the Devil's, if you dare.
>
> A straight road has no radius,
> our Father, not Domine Deus,
> America's horizon,
> royal Spanish lines is designed on:
> fly ship, swing star, navigator,
> new found land will come later,
> scribe that white page,
> hold up old Atlas, our new age.

ALL: [*Sing*]

> The world spins, argue the sun is still,
> climb into Eden by stairs of Will,
> dispute, defy your own destiny,
> ask Christ to list what he's done for thee:
> which builder raised up in hell?
> Whose tongue is hung in the leper's bell?
> Go find thy gate.
> Chance is the latch, the hinges fate.

[*Exit CHRYSOSTOM and CICELY. Enter RICHARD.*]

RICHARD: You wanted to see me?

ELIZABETH: We have things to talk about.

RICHARD: Elizabeth, I am genuinely sorry. I know how you must feel.

ELIZABETH: Save your sympathy. I can cope. What I want to know is where we go from here?

RICHARD: I will arrange a state funeral, Frank will see to it...

LOVELL: Christ, no! That's the last thing we need.

ELIZABETH: He's right, Richard. The rumour was always that you had killed Edward. Now he's dead, while in your care. Think about it.

McMASTERS: You'd be playing straight into Tudor's hands.

RICHARD: Obviously there will be repercussions, but I'll just have to weather the storm.

LOVELL: It is a storm which will drive you from the throne.

RICHARD: There is no alternative. I will simply tell the truth. He can be examined by physicians...

McMASTERS: Sire, it wouldn't work. At a time when the people must start believing in you, trusting you, admitting the boy's death would be madness. It's out of the question.

ELIZABETH: I have a suggestion to make. Richard, I want Henry Tudor to marry my daughter, in case he beats you this summer —which is a gamble, but he could, it's a calculated risk—don't shake your head, as a soldier you must know the chances of war. But to marry my daughter, Tudor must have her made legitimate. If she is legitimate, the boys are legitimate. If the boys are legitimate they have a right to the throne. So, Henry Tudor seeks the deaths of my sons, and the hand of my daughter. That is my predicament. So, as nature has killed Edward, I will use it. But Tudor must only know Edward is dead at the *right time*. That is crucial.

RICHARD: And when is that?

ELIZABETH: When the marriage contract is signed, sealed and delivered and I have agreed to the murder of Edward and young Richard as my daughter's dowry.

LOVELL: God's teeth...

ELIZABETH: [*Blazing*] What else have I got to give? Your king has impoverished me, taken all I have in the world!

RICHARD: So young Richard must die as well?
[*Coughing off. Enter PRINCE RICHARD with a yo-yo. Crosses the stage, exits.*]

ELIZABETH: He will be dead by spring.
[*RICHARD exits.*]

LOVELL: During the break some keen lads came up with a few questions. One was—what is going to be the cost of Betrayal?

McMASTERS: What market are we aiming for? We're dealing with death, we're dealing with destiny.

LOVELL: This is a game for the family. It must be enjoyed together. Mothers and sons, husbands and wives, uncles and nephews.

McMASTERS: And games are a need. They are an interpretation of existence. There is no real choice. You must play. Betrayal is a need, a mental must. Be that strong with the dealers.
[*LOVELL, McMASTERS and ELIZABETH mime the burial. CHRYSOSTOM enters.*]

CHRYSOSTOM: They buried the dead Prince under the cellar floor of the castle. Lovell and McMasters did the dirty work. By the light of a candle an uncrowned King of England was tumbled into a muddy pit. His sceptre was a stone, his orb a pebble, his crown clay. Lovell tried to recall as much of the Mass for the

Dead as he could, having heard it often of recent years, but one part slipped his mind. I could not prompt him, being a stranger here, but it runs thus—'Brethren, we will not have you ignorant concerning those who sleep, that ye sorrow not'.

[*Enter RICHARD.*]

CHRYSOSTOM: Sire, will you sit for me?

RICHARD: Not now, Greek. I have lost my wish to be remembered.

CHRYSOSTOM: A few moments of your time.

RICHARD: I said no. I have disfigured myself.

[*CICELY enters.*]

CICELY: I demand to know where my grandson is buried!

ELIZABETH: It is better that you do not know.

CICELY: I am not addressing myself to you. Richard, why has that poor boy been shovelled away as if he were some still-born brat in a stinking village?

RICHARD: Mother, it was necessary.

CICELY: As a royal prince his body must be exposed so the people can see he is dead. It matters. It is important to them.

ELIZABETH: He is not dead.

CICELY: What is she saying?

ELIZABETH: As far as they are concerned, and as far as we are concerned, he is not dead. My son is alive.

CICELY: Stop her talking. Get her to be quiet, or go away...

ELIZABETH: He agrees with me. We have had a meeting.

CICELY: The boy is dead, I touched him myself. He is as dead as a stone.

ELIZABETH: My son is alive. I, his mother, say so. Who should know better?

CICELY: You intend to make no announcement?

RICHARD: I cannot afford to.

CICELY: You are tampering with God's truth! Alive and dead are definitions which belong to Him and Him alone.

RICHARD: Mother, no one is disputing the fact of his death, only the news...

ELIZABETH: There can be no difference. He is not dead. Not dead. We must believe that. There must be no slip-ups.

CICELY: Why are you doing this? I can't believe it.

ELIZABETH: There are good reasons for both of us.

RICHARD: It would be disastrous...

CHRYSOSTOM: For his image...

CICELY: But God, Richard, you and this bitch are enemies, enemies!

RICHARD: We must work together on this one item. If Tudor beats me and does not marry the girl, then the House of York has no part in the future. Our blood is finished.

CICELY: If it uses this logic, it deserves to be.

RICHARD: I have a sound political reason.

CHRYSOSTOM: If I might help, Madam. You do admire my art, so may I try to explain? It is a simple process. Only we are aware that the boy is dead...

ELIZABETH: Was dead.

CHRYSOSTOM: Was dead. We...seven. Outside this chamber everyone who knew of Edward's existence still believes him to be alive. So, as far as they are concerned, he is alive. That is a fact to them. Go up to any man in the street and say, is Edward, the Lord Bastard, alive? And he will say, yes. So who is right? If we believe him dead we are outnumbered numerically and philosophically.

CICELY: McMasters, throw this charlatan out!

RICHARD: Leave him. It is my mind he is explaining.

CICELY: Richard, stop this now. I do not pretend to understand how you have come to this decision, only that it is wrong...Do not dispute with God in terms beyond his reckoning...

RICHARD: There was no death.

CICELY: But there is damnation. Richard, this is my fault, my sin. Let me sort it out. Do not change this much. Stay as you are, fight properly...

RICHARD: I am going back to Westminster...

CICELY: I beg you, change your mind...

LOVELL: The King moves!

CHRYSOSTOM: Wait, I haven't got started yet!

McMASTERS: To the side, to the side!

CHRYSOSTOM: This is ridiculous. How can I work this way?

LOVELL: Richard of England passes along this road. Pull over! Make room!

[*CICELY, CHRYSOSTOM, ELIZABETH exit.*]

RICHARD: Westminster. If you are a man who conceals death, live in Westminster. Leave me.

LOVELL: There is a stack of paper-work...ambassadors, plenipotentiaries, legates...

RICHARD: I will see no one. Guard the door. Leave me alone.

[*LOVELL and McMASTERS withdraw.*]

RICHARD: Sit down. Sit down. Keep very still. Try not to move. I have an itch but by God I will not scratch it, no, not for days. There, it can stay with me. Strange how it comes and goes. Good, I can bear it. Stupid bloody man! What have I done to my child? What have I done to all children? I have killed innocence and lost my own.

[*TV chimes. Enter CICELY. Lights change.*]

CICELY: Now this is a party political broadcast on behalf of the Plantagenets. When this boy was born he nearly died, and several times afterwards. We were all very surprised that he survived. It was my opinion that this was because God was unsure of whether to have him employed in heaven, or here. In those years of uncertainty I kept Richard prepared for a transfer at any time, completely acquainted with God's ideas on most subjects, and saw to it that he was well-taught...

[*McMASTERS and LOVELL come forward.*]

McMASTERS: Boy!

RICHARD: Uncle Warwick?

McMASTERS: What is the nature of God?

RICHARD: The nature of God is good.

McMASTERS: And what is the nature of the Evil One?

RICHARD: He is...evil?

McMASTERS: Then what is the nature of Man, lying in-between?

RICHARD: He is both evil and good but can alter the quantities by will and God's grace.

McMASTERS: And where stands a King? Between God and Man or between Man and the Devil?

[*Pause*]

LOVELL: Come on, Dick, you should know this mate. We only did it last week.

RICHARD: Er...in the order of the universe a King stands as at a station betwixt Man and God, but as a protector of his people from evil, betwixt Man and the Evil One.

McMASTERS: No lad, a King stands in one place only. Between the Devil and the deep blue sea.

RICHARD: Yes, Uncle.

McMASTERS: Why is it that your friend Frank knows and you don't? Can't you keep up with him? Why should he know more about kings than you?

RICHARD: I don't know, Uncle.

McMASTERS: I'll tell you, because young Frank knows what's what, not what should be. When he grows up he may find peace in an imperfect world. Will you? Supposing that you make it, that is. Feeling well today?

RICHARD: Yes, Uncle.

McMASTERS: Your father, though ill-equipped for the job, very much wanted to be king. That ambition killed him. Your brother Edward now wants to be a king. He will ask for your help. Should you help him suffer?

RICHARD: If that is my duty.

McMASTERS: Tell him, Francis, tell the child.

LOVELL: Honour thy father until thy father is dead. Honour thy brother until thy brother is dead. When the time to be alone has come, honour thyself.

RICHARD: Yes, Frank.

CICELY: As I was saying, I saw to it that he was well-taught and well-fed, brought upt to trust his place either in heaven or here on earth. In time it became plain that God had decided to let

75

my son Richard stay with me, yet kept him of an angel's size in
readiness for some swift move, upwards. Since those early years
God has changed, grown tired, and seems much older, caring less
about the things he was wont to be passionate about, such as
death. Before this Christmas we never thought of hiding death,
no king, no common man. It would have been like trying to hide
the edge of the known world, or the shape of our souls. But now
God is old, death can go disguised, no longer naked. He agrees
with my interpretation. 'Cicely,' he said after my prayers tonight,
'a favour. Let them see me as I was. I will do a deal with you.
Richard will have forgiveness for his sin of concealment if, having
hidden death, he shows it, gloriously, splendidly, dying on my
behalf in the old way, flags flying.' I could only agree. So that is
fixed, which is a comfort. In conclusion I would remind the
public that Richard bears upon his shield in battle a white boar.
It follows then that if Richard is an hog, then Richard is a swine,
which is only an edible animal like Christ himself. [*Pause*]
Goodnight.

[*TV chimes out. CICELY exits.*]

LOVELL: Richard, may we come in?

RICHARD: Stay away from me. You are all things to all men.

LOVELL: Come on Dick, cheer up. We'll crack a bottle of wine...

RICHARD: Never again with you, Lovell.

LOVELL: Why in God's name?

RICHARD: I will not drink with the Devil.

LOVELL: Dick, I want you popular, I want you safe, I want you
rare and in demand, I want you available to all. How do you sell
such a man to a cynical world? Come on, don't take it too much
to heart. We'll live to fight another day, find the right face, hit
the right note. I'm optimistic.

McMASTERS: Sire, we have worked hard to make men love you;
suspicious, difficult, tight men with teeth-marks on their tongues.
When they buy you, what thanks do we get? It's the quality of
the goods, they say, never the sales talk. Would I be fooled by
that? But we introduced them, cultivated them, got them over the
threshhold. What is on the counter? Only the man we believe in.
[*Pause*]

RICHARD: If you are such merchants of me then I am but cargo to
this country.

McMASTERS: You'll feel better tomorrow. We can sit round and sort
the whole thing out, just as Frank saya. It's nearly midnight.
Christ, it's Christmas! The clock is striking Christmas!

RICHARD: Don't come too close. What a stench you make. No, don't
talk. I want no answers, nor do I want to smell your stinking
breath. Tell me, in confidence, are you the two men trusted by
the King? You are? How does he put up with it? Who holds his

nose? Get down on your knees. [*They obey.*] Yes, you do make an effort for the King. Obviously you love the man. Touching. Is it the fashion to keep sleep in the corners of your eyes and wink yellow? Can you hear me through the corks of wax in your ears? Look at me. Who am I? Don't answer or your teeth will fall out. I am King Richard and I order you to wash. If I ever find you in such a filthy condition again I will have you scorched like a pig's carcass. Get out!

McMASTERS: You abuse me for no reason I can understand.

RICHARD: That is why I abuse you. Get out!

LOVELL: Does the death of one boy matter that much?
    [*Pause*]

RICHARD: Who was it asked me to handle a boy's death better? Oh, be this way, be that way. Now again. Are you an expert, Frank? Clot, get out!
    [*LOVELL and McMASTERS take off their surcoats.*]

LOVELL: There is a problem with this game.

McMASTERS: Some people take it too seriously.

LOVELL: They get too involved, too worked up. The manufacturers of Monopoly were blamed by businessmen for suicides amongst their less gifted children...and players who landed on Park Lane with three hotels despaired and died.

McMASTERS: Only last year we had trouble with the Big Brother game when a trade unionist threw himself from the top of Transport House after an all-night session in which he admitted to the Thought Police that although he loved humanity he could not stand the workers.

LOVELL: As you will see from the top of the box we disclaim all responsibility for accidents, but see to it that retailers are warned.

McMASTERS: Do not sell Betrayal to the over-impressionable.

LOVELL: Our games are based on great movements of thought, so they do provoke an emotional response. Just as Monopoly plays with capitalism, and Big Brother plays with socialism, Betrayal plays with humanism. And what could be more explosive? But lose the game, don't lose yourself.
    [*RICHARD cries out.*]

RICHARD: No!

McMASTERS: There he goes again.

LOVELL: The kind of child who throws the chess-pieces.

RICHARD: No!

McMASTERS: No cool. No self-control, no objective eye.

LOVELL: The game disappears. It has become too real for safety. At this point the customers should pack it in, put it all back in the box and go to bed.
    [*Lights dim. Enter CICELY, ELIZABETH and PRINCE RICHARD. RICHARD sits down, head in hands.*]

CICELY, ELIZABETH and PRINCE RICHARD: [*Sing*]

> Lully lulla, thou little tiny child,
> bye, bye, lully lullay.

> O sisters too, how may we do
> for to preserve this day,
> this poor youngling, for whom we do sing,
> bye, bye, lully lullay.

> Herod the king in his raging,
> charged he hath this day,
> his men of might in his own sight,
> all young children to slay.

> That woe is me, poor child to thee,
> and every morn and day,
> for thy parting, neither say nor sing,
> bye, bye, lully lullay.

> Lully lulla, thou little tiny child,
> bye, bye, lully lullay.

[*CICELY, ELIZABETH and PRINCE RICHARD exit. Lights change back. Enter CHRYSOSTOM.*]

CHRYSOSTOM: Sire, I know you are troubled in your mind and wish to be alone, but I may be able to help. Will you talk to me? It will help both of us.

RICHARD: I said I was not to be disturbed.

CHRYSOSTOM: They let me through because I can explain your mind. You said so yourself, remember? Your friends are confused, they cannot understand your torment. I can. I have a trained eye for such things. I am an expert.

RICHARD: Then you're welcome, Greek. Sit down.

CHRYSOSTOM: First, relax. Unwind. Close your eyes...

RICHARD: You would not be hurt if I kept them open? Habit.

CHRYSOSTOM: As you wish. Now, King Richard, let me clarify your mood, pull aside the curtains, place your thoughts in a proper perspective. [*Pause*] Are you feeling less tense now?

RICHARD: Completely at ease.

CHRYSOSTOM: Let us analyse your problem. You are ashamed that you agreed to conceal the death of your nephew. You feel out-manoeuevered, belittled. Dame Elizabeth got the better of you. In your quaint way it seems to you that if you had killed him, that would have been easier. You could have admitted it, asked God for forgiveness, done penance, and come out of it with a clear conscience. Now, your are besmirched. The affair is messy, disgusting. There is no way to get clear of it. The boy is now rotten, and so are you. You have tried blaming others but it doesn't work. It always comes back to you. You have cracked.

Now, no self-respect. Why? Because your mind is hide-bound, struggling with a new concept: state control. A king must govern the truth as if it were an unruly and rebellious citizen. Are you following me?

RICHARD: All the way. With great interest. Continue.

CHRYSOSTOM: Your brother Edward, the King before you, would have handled it better. He was in advance of his time. He could step back, get an over-all view, and manipulate his resources, and his mistakes. You are far too subjective, and that makes you a very difficult case as you are also chronically old-fashioned. Keeping up with the times imposes an enormous strain on you—your brain bulges, feels as if it will burst. But if you persevere, your nature will change. The human mind has a tremendous capacity for making adjustments under pressure. I think you will come out of this experience a better king, and a better man.

RICHARD: More like Edward.

CHRYSOSTOM: Yes. He is a good model. If you imitate him you will not go far wrong.

RICHARD: As his younger brother I tried to. I only stopped at Amiens.

CHRYSOSTOM: Amiens? His greatest achievement. A text-book example of how the Good Prince operates. Amiens is the best illustration of the new statecraft I can think of. Brilliant. What a splendid way to win a war. Such imagination and flair.

McMASTERS: King Edward went to France in 1475 to reclaim the ancient territories of the English throne...[*Exits*]

LOVELL: His young brother Richard by his side, champing at the bit. [*Exits*]

CHRYSOSTOM: Try and remember it, sire. It was a good day for you to be at school and watch the master.

RICHARD: Remember it? Could anyone forget such an illustrious occasion?

[*Enter ELIZABETH and CICELY.*]

RICHARD, CHRYSOSTOM, ELIZABETH and CICELY: [*Sing*]
>Amiens, quelle honte,
>Amiens, quel chagrin,
>quand la paix égale
>the pay pour le pays
>la victoire sans l'honneur.
>
>Amiens, quelle honte,
>Amiens, quel chagrin,
>empire perdu!
>
>Potage is French stew
>seasoned with shame.

Drunk in the street,
financial defeat.

Peace equals victory
minus honour.

Amiens, quelle honte,
jamais galante,
Amiens, quel chagrin,
la gloire enfin, fin, fin.

[*During the song McMASTERS and LOVELL appear as King Edward the Fourth of England and King Louis the Eleventh of France, dressed in crowns, bells, streamers and clogs, dancing. The dance is woven through the scene.*]

LOVELL: King Edward.

McMASTERS: King Louis.

LOVELL: What do you want?

McMASTERS: France.

LOVELL: Naked aggression.

McMASTERS: Legitimate claim.

LOVELL: Pope mediate?

McMASTERS: Your friend, not mine.

LOVELL: Single combat?

McMASTERS: No insurance.

LOVELL: Chivalry?

McMASTERS: Good books, nice pictures.

LOVELL: What is the size of your army?

McMASTERS: Twelve thousand five hundred.

LOVELL: Ah-ha, you have superior numbers. I am in trouble with my traditional allies, have rebellions at home, am not properly equipped. Under pressure I ask, combien, how much?

McMASTERS: How much? How much? What an insult! How dare you! Unthinkable. My reputation—the best general in Europe. Played nine, won nine. How much, indeed. Preposterous. What kind of man are you? You disgrace the whole idea of kingship, honour. You should be thoroughly ashamed of yourself. A hundred thousand pounds.

LOVELL: Execrable.

McMASTERS: Reasonable. And seventy-five thousand a year for life.

LOVELL: Rapacious.

McMASTERS: Inflatious. Been clipping the coinage.

LOVELL: Your problem.

McMASTERS: Now yours.

LOVELL: You are aware, I hope, that after this arrangement no English king can claim an empire in France again with any semblance of credibility? [*Pause*] I'll give you fifty thousand now and twenty-five thousand a year...

McMASTERS: No. I will not budge from my original price. Nothing will make me accept a lower offer. Eighty-nine point five now and sixty-four point five later.

LOVELL: Sixty-four point five now and thirty-nine point five...

McMASTERS: Seventy-five and fifty?

LOVELL: Done. Friend for life.

[*Exit dancing to song repeat. ELIZABETH and CICELY exit.*]

CHRYSOSTOM: And I hear you sulked in your tent like Achilles at Troy. Tut, tut, such childishness. No bloodshed, maximum profit, satisfaction to all parties, and peace. And you protested. No wonder Dame Elizabeth is so far ahead of you. As King Edward's wife she learnt by watching him at work...

RICHARD: Yes, she picks things up quickly. I am a slowcoach.

CHRYSOSTOM: You will improve. I am sure of it. With a little humility.

RICHARD: Oh, I can manage that.

CHRYSOSTOM: You are not the only king who has to make these mental adjustments. All the rulers of Europe are being forced to do likewise. You are lucky to have me here to give you these hints, I have seen it all before.

RICHARD: I realize that.

CHRYSOSTOM: You see, I am a progressive person, a new man. I have made my own way in the world, not having been born to wealth or greatness. Having come up the hard way I have discovered the colours between the lines. Life is not red and black and blue. It is orange and grey, pink and gold, a blend of blends.

RICHARD: Of course. I have never noticed the way a rainbow is made until now. How you are opening my eyes.

CHRYSOSTOM: One last thing. Don't worry about your guilty feelings. Guilt is good for you, in moderation. One could say that it is the most intense pleasure of a civilized man, but it must be controlled or you will become dependent upon it. Never be a slave to guilt.

RICHARD: I can see that I have a long way to go. Now I have doubts about whether I will ever make it to the top. You see, my most intense pleasure is that of ancient man.

CHRYSOSTOM: And what is that?

RICHARD: Pricking balloons.

CHRYSOSTOM: Pricking balloons?

RICHARD: Yes, pricking balloons like you, you fatuous trash.

CHRYSOSTOM: I see. You find my analysis inadequate.

RICHARD: No, I agree with everything you say. Why I hold you in contempt, Greek, is because you are on one side, and I am on the other. Mine may be old, but yours is decadent, and not for me! [*Exits*]

[*Enter ELIZABETH.*]

ELIZABETH: Still here? How are you finding January? Looking forward to March? May is quite mad. August? Interesting.

CHRYSOSTOM: Dame Elizabeth. You remember me?

ELIZABETH: One of the most unforgettable characters I have ever met.

CHRYSOSTOM: You are too kind. Madam, I am at my wit's end, and I am turning to you for help. I am trapped here in England. The Duchess has given orders that I am not allowed to leave the country until I have made this window of the King. He, on the other hand, will not help me. He will not keep still. He will not settle into character. It is an impossible situation for a serious artist to be in.

ELIZABETH: Dear, dear.

CHRYSOSTOM: If I was in Rome working in the Vatican...

ELIZABETH: Which you are not...

CHRYSOSTOM: Which I am not...I would breakfast with the Pope and discuss his dreams. Here I have very little status. Sometimes, in dark moments, I think that the English are barbarians, but I am never entirely convinced.

ELIZABETH: What do you want from me?

CHRYSOSTOM: Advice. Madam, I need the money from this commission. I am in debt back in Genoa, a house, a bad investment...

ELIZABETH: Why don't you do the best job you can with what you have observed so far?

CHRYSOSTOM: That is not in me. I must be useful and true to the purpose. The Duchess wants her son seen in a window, clearly. He must be transparent, all his virtues visible. I cannot do that unless I have the security of an interpretation based on a close study.

ELIZABETH: You will never get close to Richard, no one does, except his henchmen and his mother, and even if you did I doubt whether you would find him attractive.

CHRYSOSTOM: The window the Duchess wants is sheer fantasy as far as I am concerned. I see nothing admirable in the man. He is a left-over, a relic...completely out-dated...

ELIZABETH: So, you have become alienated from your subject. A difficult position for an artist to be in...

CHRYSOSTOM: I am grateful for your understanding.

ELIZABETH: Have you ever sold the same piece of work twice?

CHRYSOSTOM: On the day before an extremely long journey.

ELIZABETH: I will try to get you a second commission from a friend who is abroad at the moment. It will still be for a window of Richard, but he may want you to suggest some ideas for the basic design. Would you object to that?

CHRYSOSTOM: Not as long as I retained my...

ELIZABETH: Integrity? Of course. He would never trespass upon that. And timing will be important. He will, if he agrees to my proposal, want the window delivered at a precise moment, probably some time this summer. Would that be a problem?

CHRYSOSTOM: If I am guided towards a theme I can understand, and be made to believe in, you can have the window when you like.

ELIZABETH: Good. Now, if my idea works out and my friend puts up the money for a second commission, I think I deserve a percentage of that, don't you? How much? Ten?

CHRYSOSTOM: Five.

ELIZABETH: Seven-point-five?

CHRYSOSTOM: Done. I feel better already.

ELIZABETH: Come to think of it, I might like another portrait of myself. I could look very pleasing in glass. Edward had a painting done of me but it was very stuffy, very unimaginative. I looked quite bald and rather distant. The eyes weren't bad. Perhaps he exaggerated the eyes. We have no great sense of beauty here. I wonder why?

CHRYSOSTOM: I think it is the weather.

ELIZABETH: It can be a depressing country to live in.

CHRYSOSTOM: Yet your life has been so adventurous. You have a reputation for style, dignity, pride, beauty. You are greatly admired abroad, a new woman, the first English queen with a European mind... [*ELIZABETH smiles, remains still as if studying herself in a mirror.*] A splendid subject for a promising painter I know. The lady with the mystic smile, the I-know-it-all-but-I'm-saying-nothing smile. Right up his street. Just his kind of female. We met in Milan when I was doing my window for the Sforzas, and I said to him, Leonardo, why don't you concentrate on graphics and put aside—eschew, I said, eschew—your crackpot schemes for flying machines and submarines and parachutes? He turned to me, and with a debonair and good-natured smile replied—why don't you go and multiply yourself?

ELIZABETH: *Au revoir*, Greek. Keep in touch. Well, look at that. Catkins already.

[*Enter CICELY and RICHARD with letters.*]

RICHARD: Hello, Elizabeth. We have a surprise for you.

ELIZABETH: A surprise? I love surprises.

CICELY: A letter from abroad. We thought you'd want to read it straight away. [*Hands ELIZABETH a letter.*]

ELIZABETH: How thoughtful of you. I wonder who it could be from? [*She exits.*]

RICHARD: [*To CHRYSOSTOM*] And what are you still doing here?

CHRYSOSTOM: Trying to see you.

CICELY: Oh speak to him, Richard...

RICHARD: Will you stop hounding me? Go away.

CHRYSOSTOM: What have you got to hide? Do you think that no man can understand you? Listen, I have made men transparent with more tangles in their souls than you will ever have. You know what's the matter with you? You are afraid of the truth. What kind of a king is that?

RICHARD: Once I warned you to watch your tongue. Now watch your head.

CHRYSOSTOM: Madam, I must surrender this commission!

CICELY: You will honour that contract. Now more than ever. Break it and I will have your life. He must be remembered, he must.

CHRYSOSTOM: Why me? Find another.

CICELY: I have tried them all. Malory, here, I said, is a true knight of the Round Table, write a poem, an epic poem...sorry, no time, back to Sir Lancelot, fables, lies...Skelton, Dunbar, anyone, but no—not a wise move to eternalize such an insecure king. Italian sculptors, Flemish painters, the same reply. You are my last chance and I will not release you. When you have finished you can go where you like.

CHRYSOSTOM: Then, if he will not talk to me I will have to ask his friends. They must have some idea of what he is like. Whom should I ask?

RICHARD: [Sings]

> I am a man who makes few friends
> and that's the pity of me,
> the men I've loved have all been small,
> prepared to smile within my shadow,
> at games they gave me hidden handicaps
> and granted secret mercies,
> not knowing how I would not need them
> in this, my later lonely life.
>
> So join my friends and be
> my close companion, be one
> of this small knot I've tied
> around my heart. Intersect this circle
> and expand it to a light crown's rim
> so when you see me riding from afar
> you rise and call, that's him, that's him,
> in this my later lonely life.

[Exit RICHARD, CHRYSOSTOM, CICELY. Enter McMASTERS in his 1984 overalls.]

McMASTERS: [In a Welsh accent] I, Henry Tudor, while waiting on the coast of France for a fair wind to carry my invasion fleet to Wales, had news of Richard Plantagenet's state of mind from my future mother-in-law...

[*Enter ELIZABETH.*]

ELIZABETH: Well beloved friend, I recommend me and my daughter
to you, desiring heartily to hear of your welfare, and, if it please
you to hear of our welfare, we are not in good health of body nor
of heart, nor shall be till we hear from you. As for intelligence,
the Monster is still in disarray but come with all speed I pray
you for he ordains new regiments on every chance. On your
setting forth, which good report I pray for daily, bring with you
such tall men as may repair the fortunes of this kingdom in haste,
and, I beseech you, when your worshipful desires shall be
accomplished, let the Monster not be exempted from his fate, but
suffer it in all severity. Here, I send you this letter, asking that
my hand be not seen of none other earthly creature, save only
yourself. Yours, Elizabeth Woodville. P.S. The Monster has taken
up hawking and sends envoys all over the land looking for the
best hunting birds. It is said that he seeks better health this way,
but I trust in God that he may never find it.

McMASTERS: Hawking? Well, it will keep him from my business.
And how are your boys? Well I hope. The winters are milder
over here...

[*Exit McMASTERS and ELIZABETH. Enter RICHARD and
LOVELL with bird-whistlers on strings, swinging them round.
PRINCE RICHARD is with them, a mimed hawk on his wrist.
LOVELL is in 1484 costume.*]

RICHARD: Smell that air. Come on boy, enjoy the sunshine. The
clouds have parted. You can see for miles.

PRINCE RICHARD: I can't, it hurts my eyes to look up.

RICHARD: A Plantagenet who cannot look at the sun? Never. Stare
it out. Like me. Right in the eye.

LOVELL: There's a pigeon, two! Up with him boy!

PRINCE RICHARD: I can't, he won't let go.

LOVELL: Now they've gone. You were too slow.

RICHARD: What do you call this clinging hawk, boy.

PRINCE RICHARD: Bacillus, uncle. Bacillus.

LOVELL: Larks, there, finches, wrens and robins...loose him!

RICHARD: Up, Bacillus, up!

PRINCE RICHARD: [*Struggling with the hawk*] He won't leave me...

LOVELL: God's teeth boy, beat him, thrust him from you!

RICHARD: There's a smug, speckled thrush! There's a well-fed bird
if ever I saw one! Attack! Burst him like a bladder!

PRINCE RICHARD: [*Fighting with the hawk*] He's pecking me!
He's eating me!

[*RICHARD and LOVELL still watch the sky, turning their bird-
whistlers as PRINCE RICHARD struggles with the hawk.*]

LOVELL: What a day, what a wild spring day. Remember?

85

RICHARD: The moors and that enormous northern sky...

PRINCE RICHARD: He's eating me, uncle, uncle...

LOVELL: A place to get lost in...

RICHARD: For days you would never see another soul. Frank, if I could have the north for my own, I would gladly surrender the rest of this nation. There are a hundred years of the old ways left up there.

PRINCE RICHARD: Help me! My throat, my throat...[*He falls to the ground, still fighting the hawk. Dies.*]

LOVELL: Who will you trust your armies to when the time comes?

McMASTERS: [*Still as Henry Tudor*] I'm listening, I'm listening...

RICHARD: Norfolk...

LOVELL: Good...

RICHARD: Northumberland...

LOVELL: No, not him. Not a Percy, they've always been Lancastrian. That's asking to be let down.

RICHARD: Isn't it. And Stanley.

[*Pause*]

LOVELL: You expect me to ride with you and him in the same cause?

RICHARD: If that cause is me.

[*Pause*]

LOVELL: And how are we going to pay for this campaign? The Treasury is as empty as a scraped plate. We cannot offer security for your debts...

RICHARD: God must become a banker. For his own anointed he will have low interest rates.

[*Enter CICELY.*]

CICELY: I hear everything is going very well. You can expect massive support from the merchants...

LOVELL: Afterwards.

RICHARD: Don't be so glum, Frank. As if it mattered. Where did other kings get their money from?

LOVELL: They had a very effective method of boosting their foreign exchange reserves. It was a short-term policy but it had distinct advantages as it artificially stimulated cash-flow and offset their domestic taxation income deficits. It was called...plunder.

RICHARD: It was the only time when running the Exchequer was any fun at all. What do you say, mother? [*Bitterly*] Don't we need another Amiens?

CICELY: Don't be flippant, Richard. Those days are over.

CICELY, RICHARD: [*Sing*]

> The England that was here has gone
> its song was that of Lion and Swan
> its colours gules now crimson,

[*Enter ELIZABETH.*]

ALL: [*Sing*]   astute men hid beneath the lid
of helmet, casque and basinet
to see what plunder they could get,
a sound financial reason:
the Bull, the Fiery Cresset, Goat,
put on a steel and leather coat
and sharpened lance and sword,
then struck their tent
and went hell-bent
with blood upon their blazon.
Were Exeter and Bedford, Beaufort,
Somerset and Gloucester out for
any more than he who smashes grapes
to hurry on a raisin?
Can you tell me that Talbot, Percy,
Neville, Howard, loved the Lord of mercy
more than loot?
Then let me tell you economics
was of old England's foreign policy
the branch and stem and root.
So now the boys are dead, the summer grass
grows high above accountants' heads
in Aquitaine and sweet Champagne,
Anjou, Bordeaux and Agincourt,
while we are left with penniless regret and spend
        our time
devising systems of respectable extortion of a
        different sort.

[*Exit CICELY and RICHARD. Enter CHRYSOSTOM.*]

ELIZABETH: Do you find the offer acceptable? Practicable?

CHRYSOSTOM: I will need protection...the Duchess will not be pleased. I appear, in my honesty as an artist, to have compromised myself.

ELIZABETH: The Duchess will be a nobody after this summer. You have nothing to fear from her...

CHRYSOSTOM: You mentioned instructions...

ELIZABETH: Yes...come closer [*Whispers in CHRYSOSTOM's ear.*]

CHRYSOSTOM: Well, at least it is...positive. I'm exhausted with trying to find my own interpretation. I am not happy to accept a client's dictation in these matters, but...beggars must.

ELIZABETH: Do a good job and the Tudor may bring you back to do more...simple people.

[*ELIZABETH and CHRYSOSTOM exit. McMASTERS comes forward. LOVELL has taken off his surcoat and changes to 1984.*]

LOVELL: It's here that the designers of Betrayal have inserted their hook, their special selling feature. Here, just before Bosworth, every player left in the game draws a card from a reserve pack. Imagine, a late night, the bottle almost finished, the fire dying down...then, something truly terrifying...real forfeits, hard-hitting forfeits. It's a lot of fun, a bundle of laughs. The losing players, this being a tightly-controlled, highly-managed game of dynamic relationships, must cough up. You can lose...

McMASTERS: [*Welsh accent*] Life. Reputation. Respect. Affection. Existence in any real past. Once dead, Dick will be part of my package for the new age. The part that is perforated, ripped along the dotted line, and out of which my genius will pour like freely-flowing salt. I will recreate him.

LOVELL: Tough. But necessary if Henry Tudor as the winner is to consolidate his victory and be seen as the nation's deliverer from a reign of terror. Claim to the throne—nil. Blow that cobweb away. But full marks for opportunism, drive, planning, energy and...here lies his greatest innovation in advertising—selling by the negative.

McMASTERS: Buy this because your old game was dangerous...

LOVELL: Inflammable...

McMASTERS: Got stuck in the kid's windpipe...

LOVELL: An inferior product in every way. Never realized it? Baby, you'd never thought about it. Where's Ludo now? See any Snakes and Ladders?

McMASTERS: He was the grandaddy of us all and, like us, knew himself in the Greek way, and was always aware of what he was doing. In our profession, is anyone unsure of who is father, who is child? Henry Tudor wasn't, and neither are we, are we boys? To sell, you have to think you are the father and the customer is the child.

LOVELL, McMASTERS: [*Sing*]

> Baby, baby,
> who's calling you baby?
> Baby, baby,
> who's calling you child?
> Mind is mental
> truth's on a rental,
> suck this, see this
> game's driving me wild.

[*CHRYSOSTOM and CICELY enter.*]

CHRYSOSTOM: Madam. I have it. The window. May I continue? I would like to deliver the goods, do the work. Please say yes. Sorry for the delay.

CICELY: You may be too late. The Tudor has already set sail from Harfleur. Richard will be going north...gathering his army.

CHRYSOSTOM: Will he come here?

CICELY: I have asked him to, to say goodbye...
CHRYSOSTOM: And good luck?
CICELY: Hear that, God? [*Chuckles*] Poor man, make your window.
LOVELL: McMASTERS, CICELY: [*Sing*]

> Baby, baby,
> who's calling you baby?
> Baby, baby,
> your style's infantile,
> choice and chunky
> you sweet little monkey,
> got your number
> down here on my file.

[*Enter RICHARD with ELIZABETH.*]
ELIZABETH: Resistance is pointless, Richard. You haven't got a
  chance now. All your generals have been bought and sold.
RICHARD: Is your daughter well?
ELIZABETH: Excellent health. Looking forward to being a bride.
RICHARD: Virgin?
ELIZABETH: I beg your pardon!
RICHARD: It was a thought. Has England ever had a virgin queen?
LOVELL, McMASTERS, CICELY and ELIZABETH: [*Sing*]

> Baby, baby,
> who's calling you baby?
> Baby, baby,
> your mouth is too wide.
> Double tissue,
> oh how I miss you,
> deep, absorbent,
> thick, tender pile.

CICELY: Have you finished yet, Greek? Richard is only hours away.
CHRYSOSTOM: Not long now. Just the final touches, a quick polish
  and everything will be ready.
CICELY: Is it beautiful?
CHRYSOSTOM: It works superbly. It is strikingly effective.
CICELY: Has it meaning?
CHRYSOSTOM: It is all meaning. It is the significant future.
CICELY: Will it last?
CHRYSOSTOM: For ever, and ever, and ever, Amen. [*Aside*] And
  paid for twice. [*Exits*]
ELIZABETH: And what are you going to leave behind? What
  testament?
RICHARD: I have left my will blank. Have you learnt to write?
ELIZABETH: What a death you contemplate. So empty.
RICHARD: Not empty, clean. A clean break with the past.

ALL: [*Sing*]   Baby, baby,
                who's calling you baby?
                Baby, baby,
                your daddy has died.
                Joker Jesus no longer deceives us,
                kings and countries
                admit they have lied.

                No replacement
                to your amazement,
                substitution, never designed.
                Lost and lonely,
                the future is phoney,
                sad and simple
                to battle you ride.

CICELY: Richard, welcome back to Berkhamsted.

RICHARD: Mother, you asked me to call.

CICELY: Richard, God has promised me that I will be the last survivor. I will see it all, the change, the rolling away of my times. Won't that be wonderful? And I will be aware. I won't lose my faculties. No second childhood for Cicely. He is saying, you kept this machine going, and when it stops it can stand in your back garden and rust. Isn't that like him? A sense of what is absolutely right...

RICHARD: I can't stay long.

CICELY: I have a surprise for you. Remember last Christmas?

RICHARD: I have been trying to forget it.

CICELY: Richard, the Greek says that he has found his theme and made something marvellous of it. I have resisted the temptation to look in order to share this moment with you. [*Pause*] Quiet, please. I have a few words to say. King Richard has given up some of his precious time—the land is in a crisis as you know—to be with us here today...

RICHARD: Mother, shall we get on with it?

CICELY: This window is for my son, and God, the only two men worth talking to as far as I am concerned. It is a gift to the present, and the future, made from the past. It comes with love from mother.

RICHARD: Thank you. [*Kisses her.*] It was a nice thought. Where do I stand? Here? Will this do? Really, I would have thought it better left aside...however, if it will please you. Right. Short speech. Usual thing. All set? What a waste of money. [*Pause*] We do not know what is behind this curtain, and we never will. We turn our backs upon it and go our own way north, to fight. If it helps you, my people, to look upon another man's image of us, then that is his profit, not ours. We do not consider him necessary. Do not look upon us as ungenerous for this attitude—we know who we are, where we are fixed. We do not have to be interpreted as this King speaks good English. [*Pause*] There are things which we have to do, men we must meet, arrangements we must make. We have little time left. Let us get it over with.

[*Enter CHRYSOSTOM in a snappy modern suit, carrying a brief-case. He shakes LOVELL's and McMASTERS's hands and kisses LOUISE's with an elegant mocking bow.*]

CHRYSOSTOM: You cannot satisfy all of your customers all of the time. You must choose your market, build up a good complaints department, and smile.

[*CHRYSOSTOM sits down at the chess-table.*]

RICHARD: We do not accept this picture of us. It was made by an alien mind from an alien age and it cannot be right. After you have seen it, remember that we have remained ourselves and nothing will ever alter that. This window is a game in glass, played upon our living years. It is artificial. It is false!

CICELY: Three cheers for God! Hip-hip-hooray! Hip-hip-hooray! Hip-hip-hooray! Let's see it, let's see it!

RICHARD: Unveil the window. I refuse to look.

[*McMASTERS and LOVELL pull back the Betrayal board curtains. Blackout. The window flares up in brilliant primary colours. It is a savage political cartoon of RICHARD killing and eating children. CICELY falls to the ground. Lights up.*]

CICELY: No, no, that's not him...

CHRYSOSTOM: Like any artist of note, I can accept criticism of my work. I'm interested in how people react to what I put before them. This window? Well, it was done for money and to get me out of England. Justify it? It's useful, oh yes. Here, in this backward village of Berkhamsted there is a positive sigh of relief. My window pin-points evil for them, provides an answer to the old problem of who to blame for the past and who not to trust for the future. It legislates against confusion and acts as signpost to a better, brighter age.

RICHARD: It is not me. It is not me. It is not me.

[*CHRYSOSTOM takes the bag with the chess-pieces out of his brief-case and empties it on to the chess-table, then sets up the game, giving himself the black. CICELY gets up.*]

ALL: [*Sing*] Collect all the pieces
put the game in the drawer,
tonight is tonight,
the fact is not law,
green goes to amber,
amber to red,
the child in his dream
is the child in his bed.

Are you aware what you're doing to me?
Who asked you? Who asked you?
the dream of the child,
the child unaware,
the fear of the future
when the game isn't there.

RICHARD: [*Sings*]
Are you aware of what you're doing to me?
Who asked you? Who asked you?
Subliminal images of history,
Who asked you? Who asked you?
There's no chance you're going to get me right,
I see me, and you see sight!
Are you aware of what you're doing to me?
Who asked you? Who asked you?

ALL: [*Sing*]   Are you aware of what you're doing to me?
Who asked you? Who asked you?
The dreams of the child, green goes to amber,
the child unaware, amber to red,
the child in his dreams, the fear of the future,
the child in his bed, when the game isn't there.

RICHARD: [*Sings*]
Are you aware of what you're doing to me?
Who asked you? Who asked you?
Has anyone here ever heard
of a whore called Historical Accuracy?
If you bump into her give her a message
from dead Richard Three,
say I hope she gets better publicity
than me.

ALL: [*Sing*]   Are you aware of what you're doing to me?
Who asked you? Who asked you?
Are you aware of what you're doing to me?
Who asked you? Who asked you?

LOVELL: Fade the lights, Louise. The evenings are early in the
north.
[*RICHARD, ELIZABETH, McMASTERS and LOVELL exit.
CICELY is standing in front of the window in a cold pool of
light.*]
CICELY: This is how my son died. On the battlefield he was deserted
by two of his generals and his army melted away. At the head of
only a hundred men he charged the enemy and cut his way
through to the feet of Henry Tudor himself, killing his standard-

bearer. But his momentum had been absorbed by greater numbers and they closed around him and he was slain. His naked body was slung over a horse and taken to Leicester where it was exposed in the market-place so that the people might see he was dead. Friars from a nearby religious house had to beg for his body in order to give it a decent burial. Later, his bones were dug up and thrown into the river. That he would have been grateful for as I cannot see him resting easy in the earth of this new England. The river suited him better. [*Exits*]

[*Enter ORWELL in his dressing-gown and pyjamas. He goes over to the table and stands by it.*]

CHRYSOSTOM: Another game? Will you be more in control of yourself this time?

[*ORWELL nods, sits down to the white side.*]

CHRYSOSTOM: Oh, I have something for you. [*Brings a book out of his brief-case.*] Your advance copy of *1984*. Looks good. [*Puts it on the table by ORWELL's hand.*] Certainly nothing to be ashamed of.

[*Pause*] Your move I think.

[*Pause. ORWELL knocks over his king.*
Blackout.]

NOTES ON THE MUSIC

Where background or incidental music is indicated, the theme from 'Peace is man's richest possession' (at the end of 'No one knows but the Lord') can be used; e.g. during the Danube Room scene early in Act One and at the beginning of Act Two.

'Sir, Emperor, Lord of all the ground'. The accompaniment can be extended after the song for Chrysostom's dance.

'Lully, lulla'. The music for 'The Coventry Carol' (original version) can be found in the *Oxford Book of Carols*, No. 22.

'Amiens'. The verses and instrumental breaks to which the kings dance should be interspersed with the dialogue of the scene.

'Baby, baby'. The guitar accompaniment may be played beneath the scenes linking the verses.

Instruments used in the original production included rebec, crumhorn, Nordic lyre, Appalachian dulcimer and psaltery—as well as guitar and electric piano. However, other instruments of comparable pitch may be substituted. This is only an outline of the score, the full version of which may be obtained by applying in the first instance to:
John Johnson, Clerkenwell House, 45-47 Clerkenwell Green, London EC1R 0HT.

Reproductions

Sir, Emperor Lord of all the ground

WORDS TRADITIONAL, ADAPTED BY DAVID POWNALL

This figure repeated throughout the piece.

CHRYSOSTOM:

Sir, Empe-ror Lord of all the ground,

High Prince, son of a no-ble house, You must give up your gol-den

a-pple, your blade, scep-tre, Your trea-sure trove And with all dance my

way Hol-ding hands with A-dam's chil-dren as they go.

Some go-ing quick, some go- ing slow.

When you look on this shell The gest-ure in an an-tique

dance See what you are and where your na-ture leads, Food for

worms, un-in-sta-ted trash, With on-ly words and dead sons for re-mem-brance

Here he sits who is a king, A-live but

dead, a doomed, in-an-i-ma-ted thing

I have ne-ver learnt to dance with hope But on-ly at the mass with sa-vage

steps Who is the hum-blest is the most wise, The king would be

be-tter with a dan-cer's eyes

Child

RICHARD (BOY):
Child means a man with-out beard or voice Child means a man with-out mor-tal fears.

ELIZABETH:
Child means a wo-man who will re-joice Child means a woman in la-bours tears.

CICELY:
Don't ad-mire the un-lit fire the ab-sent flame, The play-er who is not yet rea-dy for the game, Save your re-spect, try to pro-tect the i-deal of a-dult, And when you find the per-fect power, ex-ult, ex-ult.

RICHARD:
Child means the me of yes-ter-day, Child is the per-son who haunts my bones

ELIZABETH:
Child is the bird in the month of May, Child is the night-mares moans and groans.

CHORUS:
Child means an ar-gu-ment in age, Child means a feat of me-mo-ry. Child means a bird in a hu-man cage

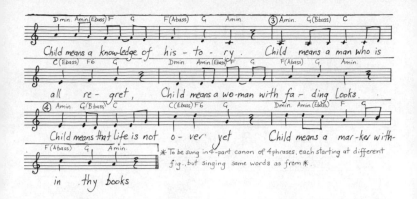

Child means a know-ledge of his-to-ry. Child means a man who is

all re-gret, Child means a wo-man with fa-ding looks.

Child means that life is not o-ver yet Child means a mar-ker with-

in thy books

* To be sung in 4-part canon of 4 phrases, each starting at different fig., but singing same words as from *.

No one knows but de Lord / Peace

The rules of the game

Take a chance card and then advance to Car- mar- then Darn it
Barn-et Try a-gain A-mi-ens, You seem to be
hea-din' for a show-down at Edin - burgh Tilt of the board
Sto-ny Strat-ford, Lu- cky man No- tting-ham
In the red Berk-ham-stead What you worth
Bos- worth? Now these are the rules of the
game Shake the dice when I call out your name Throw a
three or a four or a five, And we'll see who is
stay-ing a- Live.

The earth will not be the centre

VS.1 'THE EARTH WILL NOT BE THE CENTRE'—UPPER VOICE & ACCOMP. ONLY.

Dis- pute, de- fy your own des-ti- ny   Ask Christ to
list what he's done for thee.   Which buil- der   raised up   hell
Whose tongue is   hung in the Le-per's bell.   Go   find thy
gate   Chance   is   the   Latch the hin — ges fate.

Amiens

Unaccompanied
Brisk

A - mi - ens quelle hon - te,   A - mi-ens quel   cha - grin

quand la   paix {é ——— ga é - ga -} le

Em-   pi - {re ——— per re per —} du

Drunk in the   street {fi ——— nan - cial de -} feat
                        {fi   nan cialde} feat

1.
The

pay   pour le pays, la vic- toire sans l'honn-eur.   The

pay pour le pays la vic — toire sans l'honn-eur.

Po-tage is French Stew sea-soned with shame

Po-tage is French Stew sea-soned with shame

Peace e-quals vic-tory mi-nus ho-nour. Peace e-quals vic-tory

mi-nus ho-nour

A-mi-ens quelle hon-te ja-mais ga-

llan-te. A-mi-ens quel cha-grin. La

gloire en-fin, fin, fin.

I am a man who makes few friends

The England that was here has gone

Baby, baby

crisp & animato

LOVELL & McMASTERS:

D / / E A E / A

1. Ba-by, ba-by, who's call-ing you ba-by.

F#min. / E A E / F#min.

Ba-by, ba-by who's call-ing you child.

D / E A E / A

Mind is men-tal, truth's on a ren-tal.

F#min. / E A E / F#min.

ELIZABETH, L., MTM. & CICELY: Suck this, see this, game's dri-ving me wild.

D / E A E / A

*
4. Ba-by, ba-by, who's call-ing you ba-by,
F#min. / E A E / F#min.

Ba-by, ba-by, your Da-ddy has died.
D / E' A E / A

Jo-ker Je-sus no Lon-ger de- ceives us
F#min. / E A E / F#min.

ALL: Kings and count-ries ad- mit that they have lied
D / A E F#min. Bmin.

5. No re-place-ment to your a- maze- ment.
F#min. / / E A E F#min.

Sub-sti- tu- tion ne- ver de- signed
D / A E F#min. Bmin.

Lost and lone-ly, the fu- ture is pho- ney
F#min. / / E A E A Db/ f.nstr.

Sad and sim-ple to bat-tle you ride.

* Verse 2 — tune + lower part.
Verses 3 & 4 — all three parts

Collect all the pieces

fear of the fu-ture when the game is-n't

dream is the child in his bed

there Are you a-ware of what you're do-ing to me, Who asked you, who asked you, Has

a-ny-one here e-ver heard of the whore called his-to-ri-cal a-ccu-ra-cy If you bump

in-to her, give her a me-ssage from dead Ri-chard

three, Say I hope she gets be-tter pub-li-ci-ty than

me Are you a-ware of what you're do-ing to me, Who asked you, who asked you

me Are you a-ware of what you're do-ing to me, Who asked you, who asked you.